ABBREVIATIONS

alt	=	alternate
mm	=	millimeter(s)
cm	=	centimeter(s)
in(s)	=	inch(es)
g	=	gram(s)
beg	=	beginning
alt	=	alternate
st(s)	=	stitch(es)
inc	=	increase
dec	=	decrease
0	=	no sts, times or rows
K	=	knit
P	=	purl
tog	=	together
cont	=	continue(ity)
rep	=	repeat
rem	=	remaining
rnd	=	round
sl	=	slip
pat	=	pattern
psso	=	pass slipped st over
yo	=	yarn over
Sl1K	=	slip next st knitwise
Sl1P	=	slip next st purlwise

* = The star symbol is a repeat sign and means that you follow the printed instructions from the first * until you reach the second *. You will then repeat from * to * the given number of times which **does not** include the first time. The ** and *** are used in the same way.

[ ] = Brackets mean that the enclosed instructions are to be worked the number of times stated after the brackets.

Work even = Work without increasing or decreasing in the established pattern.

YARN

The items shown can be made with any yarn in the weight specified as long as the correct gauge can be obtained.
It is best to refer to the yardage to determine how many skeins to purchase.

GAUGE

Remember, in order for your item to be the correct size, it is not the brand of yarn that matters, but the GAUGE that is important.

Exact gauge is **essential** for proper fit. Before beginning your item, make a sample swatch using the yarn and needle specified. After completing the swatch, measure it, counting your stitches and rows carefully. If your swatch is larger or smaller than specified, **make another, changing needle size to get the correct gauge.** Keep trying until you find the size needles that will give you the specified gauge. Once proper gauge is obtained, measure width of item approximately every 3" to be sure gauge remains consistent.

Note: Never put an iron directly on yarns containing synthetic fibers. If pressing is required before assembly, lay each piece right side down on a clean, flat surface and pin to size using rust proof pins. Cover with a damp cloth and leave to dry.

Pattern Ratings

Easy	Means an easy knit. This includes knit and purl stitches with some basic increasing and decreasing.
Intermediate	Means an average knit. These require some specialized knowledge, such as color block, fair isle or aran techniques. They may also require the ability to keep continuity of simple pattern stitches during shaping.
Advanced	Means a challenge knit. These will require the ability to keep continuity of pattern stitches during shaping and may combine several different techniques.
Expert	These require an extra degree of patience and skill.

1. Just Like Mom

Intermediate

SIZES

Chest/bust measurement

6	25"
8	26½"
10	28"
Extra-Small	32"
Small	34"
Medium	36"
Large	38"
Extra-Large	40"

Finished chest/bust

6	33"
8	36"
10	39"
Extra-Small	42"
Small	44½"
Medium	47"
Large	49½"
Extra-Large	52"

Size Note: *Instructions are written for size 6, with sizes 8, 10, Extra-Small, Small, Medium, Large, and Extra-Large in braces { }. Instructions will be easier to read if you circle all the numbers pertaining to your size. If only one number is given, it applies to all sizes.*

MATERIALS

Worsted Weight Yarn: 3½ oz (223 yds/100 g)

Sizes	6	8	10	XS	S	M	L	XL	
	4	5	5	6	7	8	8	9	balls

Samples made with **Patons Classic Merino Wool.**

Sizes 6 (4 mm) and 7 (4.5 mm) knitting needles **or size needed for gauge.** Cable needle.

GAUGE SWATCH

20 sts and 26 rows = 4" with larger needles in stocking st.

STITCH GUIDE

MB = [(K1. P1) twice. K1] into next st. Pass 4th, 3rd, 2nd and 1st sts separately over 5th st. Bobble complete.
Cr3L = slip next 2 sts onto a cable needle and leave at front of work. P1, then K2 from cable needle.
Cr3R = slip next st onto a cable needle and leave at back of work. K2, then P1 from cable needle.
Cr4L = slip next 3 sts onto a cable needle and leave at front of work. P1, then K3 from cable needle.
Cr4R = slip next st onto a cable needle and leave at back of work. K3, then P1 from cable needle.
C4F = slip next 2 sts onto a cable needle and leave at front of work. K2, then K2 from cable needle.
C4B = slip next 2 sts onto a cable needle and leave at back of work. K2, then K2 from cable needle.
C6F = slip next 3 sts onto a cable needle and leave at front of work. K3, then K3 from cable needle.
C6B = slip next 3 sts onto a cable needle and leave at back of work. K3, then K3 from cable needle.
M1 = pick up horizontal loop lying before next st and knit into back of it.

PANEL PAT A (worked over 21 sts – *see chart on page 7*).

Foundation row 1: (Right Side). P3. K2. P6. K2. P2. MB. P3. K2.

Foundation row 2: Knit all knit sts and purl all purl sts as they appear.

Proceed in pat as follows:

1st row: (Right Side). P3. K2. P6. K2. (P1. MB) twice. P2. K2.

2nd and following alt rows: Knit all knit sts and purl all purl sts as they appear.

3rd row: P3. Cr3L. P4. Cr3R. P2. MB. P3. K2.
5th row: P4. Cr3L. P2. Cr3R. P6. Cr3R.
7th row: P2. MB. P2. Cr3L. Cr3R. P6. Cr3R. P1.
9th row: (P1. MB) twice. P2. C4F. P6. Cr3R. P2.
11th row: P2. MB. P2. Cr3R. Cr3L. P4. Cr3R. P3.
13th row: P4. Cr3R. P2. Cr3L. P2. Cr3R. P4.
15th row: P3. Cr3R. P4. Cr3L. Cr3R. P2. MB. P2.
17th row: P2. Cr3R. P6. C4B. P2. (MB. P1) twice.
19th row: P1. Cr3R. P6. Cr3R. Cr3L. P2. MB. P2.
21st row: Cr3R. P6. Cr3R. P2. Cr3L. P4.
23rd row: K2. P3. MB. P2. Cr3R. P4. Cr3L. P3.
25th row: K2. P2. (MB. P1) twice. K2. P6. K2. P3.
27th row: K2. P3. MB. P2. Cr3L. P4. Cr3R. P3.
29th row: Cr3L. P6. Cr3L. P2. Cr3R. P4.
31st row: P1. Cr3L. P6. Cr3L. Cr3R. P2. MB. P2.
33rd row: P2. Cr3L. P6. C4B. P2. (MB. P1) twice.
35th row: P3. Cr3L. P4. Cr3R. Cr3L. P2. MB. P2.
37th row: P4. Cr3L. P2. Cr3R. P2. Cr3L. P4.
39th row: P2. MB. P2. Cr3L. Cr3R. P4. Cr3L. P3.
41st row: (P1. MB) twice. P2. C4F. P6. Cr3L. P2.
43rd row: P2. MB. P2. Cr3R. Cr3L. P6. Cr3L. P1.
45th row: P4. Cr3R. P2. Cr3L. P6. Cr3L.
47th row: P3. Cr3R. P4. Cr3L. P2. MB. P3. K2.
48th row: As 2nd row.

These 48 rows form Panel Pat A.

PANEL PAT B (worked over 24 sts– *see chart on page 7*).

Foundation row 1: (Right Side). P3. K3. P6. K3. P2. MB. P3. K3.

Foundation row 2: Knit all knit sts and purl all purl sts as they appear.

Proceed in pat as follows:

1st row: (Right Side). P3. K3. P6. K3. (P1. MB) twice. P2. K3.

2nd and following alt rows: Knit all knit sts and purl all purl sts as they appear.

3rd row: P3. Cr4L. P4. Cr4R. P2. MB. P3. K3.
5th row: P4. Cr4L. P2. Cr4R. P6. Cr4R.
7th row: P2. MB. P2. Cr4L. Cr4R. P6. Cr4R. P1.
9th row: (P1. MB) twice. P2. C6F. P6. Cr4R. P2.
11th row: P2. MB. P2. Cr4R. Cr4L. P4. Cr4R. P3.
13th row: P4. Cr4R. P2. Cr4L. P2. Cr4R. P4.
15th row: P3. Cr4R. P4. Cr4L. Cr4R. P2. MB. P2.
17th row: P2. Cr4R. P6. C6B. P2. (MB. P1) twice.
19th row: P1. Cr4R. P6. Cr4R. Cr4L. P2. MB. P2.
21st row: Cr4R. P6. Cr4R. P2. Cr4L. P4.
23rd row: K3. P3. MB. P2. Cr4R. P4. Cr4L. P3.
25th row: K3. P2. (MB. P1) twice. K3. P6. K3. P3.
27th row: K3. P3. MB. P2. Cr4L. P4. Cr4R. P3.
29th row: Cr4L. P6. Cr4L. P2. Cr4R. P4.
31st row: P1. Cr4L. P6. Cr4L. Cr4R. P2. MB. P2.
33rd row: P2. Cr4L. P6. C6B. P2. (MB. P1) twice.
35th row: P3. Cr4L. P4. Cr4R. Cr4L. P2. MB. P2.
37th row: P4. Cr4L. P2. Cr4R. P2. Cr4L. P4.
39th row: P2. MB. P2. Cr4L. Cr4R. P4. Cr4L. P3.
41st row: (P1. MB) twice. P2. C6F. P6. Cr4L. P2.
43rd row: P2. MB. P2. Cr4R. Cr4L. P6. Cr4L. P1.
45th row: P4. Cr4R. P2. Cr4L. P6. Cr4L.
47th row: P3. Cr4R. P4. Cr4L. P2. MB. P3. K3.
48th row: As 2nd row.

These 48 rows form Panel Pat B.

BACK

With smaller needles, cast on 83 {**91**-99-**106**-112-**118**-124-**130**} sts.

Work in garter st (knit every row) for 3 rows, ending with **wrong side** facing for next row.

Next row: K34 {**38**-42-**43**-46-**49**-52-**55**}. (M1. K4) 4 {**4**-4-**0**-0-**0**-0-**0**} times. (K2. M1. K3) 0 {**0**-0-**4**-4-**4**-4-**4**} times. K33 {**37**-41-**43**-46-**49**-52-**55**}. 87 {**95**-103-**110**-116-**122**-128-**134**} sts.

Change to larger needles and proceed in pat as follows:
1st row: (Right Side). P23 {**27**-31-**33**-36-**39**-42-**45**}. MB. P9. Work next 21 {**21**-21-**24**-24-**24**-24-**24**} sts as foundation row 1 of Panel Pat A {**A**-A-**B**-B-**B**-B-**B**}. P9. MB. P23 {**27**-31-**33**-36-**39**-42-**45**}.
2nd row: K33 {**37**-41-**43**-46-**49**-52-**55**}. Work next 21 {**21**-21-**24**-24-**24**-24-**24**} sts as foundation row 2 of Panel Pat A {**A**-A-**B**-B-**B**-B-**B**}. K33 {**37**-41-**43**-46-**49**-52-**55**}.

Panel Pat is now in position.

Keeping cont of Panel Pat, proceed in pat as follows:
3rd row: P22 {**26**-30-**32**-35-**38**-41-**44**}. MB. P1. MB. P8. Work appropriate row of Panel Pat across next 21 {**21**-21-**24**-24-**24**-24-**24**} sts. P8. MB. P1. MB. P22 {**26**-30-**32**-35-**38**-41-**44**}.

4th and every following alt row: K33 {**37**-41-**43**-46-**49**-52-**55**}. Work appropriate row of Panel Pat across next 21 {**21**-21-**24**-24-**24**-24-**24**} sts. K33 {**37**-41-**43**-46-**49**-52-**55**}.

5th row: P23 {**27**-31-**33**-36-**39**-42-**45**}. MB. P9. Work appropriate row of Panel Pat across next 21 {**21**-21-**24**-24-**24**-24-**24**} sts. P9. MB. P23 {**27**-31-**33**-36-**39**-42-**45**}.

7th row: P33 {**37**-41-**43**-46-**49**-52-**55**}. Work appropriate row of Panel Pat across next 21 {**21**-21-**24**-24-**24**-24-**24**} sts. P33 {**37**-41-**43**-46-**49**-52-**55**}.

9th row: P7 {**11**-15-**17**-20-**23**-26-**29**}. MB. P25. Work appropriate row of Panel Pat across next 21 {**21**-21-**24**-24-**24**-24-**24**} sts. P25. MB. P7 {**11**-15-**17**-20-**23**-26-**29**}.

11th row: P6 {**10**-14-**16**-19-**22**-25-**28**}. MB. P1. MB. P24. Work appropriate row of Panel Pat across next 21 {**21**-21-**24**-24-**24**-24-**24**} sts. P24. MB. P1. MB. P6 {**10**-14-**16**-19-**22**-25-**28**}.

13th row: As 9th row.

15th row: As 7th row.

17th row: P33 {**37**-41-**2**-5-**8**-11-**14**}. (MB. P40) 0 {**0**-0-**1**-1-**1**-1-**1**} time. Work appropriate row of Panel Pat across next 21 {**21**-21-**24**-24-**24**-24-**24**} sts. (P40. MB) 0 {**0**-0-**1**-1-**1**-1-**1**} time. P33 {**37**-41-**2**-5-**8**-11-**14**}.

19th row: P33 {**37**-41-**1**-4-**7**-10-**13**}. (MB. P1. MB. P39) 0 {**0**-0-**1**-1-**1**-1-**1**} time. Work appropriate row of Panel Pat across next 21 {**21**-21-**24**-24-**24**-24-**24**} sts. (P39. MB. P1. MB) 0 {**0**-0-**1**-1-**1**-1-**1**} time. P33 {**37**-41-**1**-4-**7**-10-**13**}.

21st row: As 17th row.

23rd row: As 7th row.

24th row: As 4th row.

These 24 rows form Bobble Pat at either side of Panel Pat.

Cont in pat until Back from beg measures 12¼ {**13¾**-15-**16½**-18-**18½**-18½-**19**}", ending with right side facing for next row.

Shape armholes: Keeping cont of pat, bind off 5 {**5**-5-**6**-6-**6**-6-**6**} sts beg next 2 rows. 77 {**85**-93-**98**-104-**110**-116-**122**} sts.

Cont even in pat until armhole measures 7½ {**8¼**-9-**9½**-10-**10**-10½-**10½**}", ending with right side facing for next row.

Shape shoulders and back neck: Bind off 8 {**9**-10-**11**-11-**12**-13-**14**} sts beg next 2 rows. 61 {**67**-73-**76**-82-**86**-90-**94**} sts.

Next row: (Right Side). Bind off 8 {**9**-10-**11**-11-**12**-13-**14**} sts. Pat across until there are 11 {**13**-14-**14**-16-**17**-17-**18**} sts on right-hand needle. Turn and work this side first.

Bind off 4 sts beg next row.

Bind off rem 7 {**9**-10-**10**-12-**13**-13-**14**} sts.

With right side facing, rejoin yarn to rem sts. Bind off center 23 {**23**-25-**26**-28-**28**-30-**30**} sts, dec 4 sts evenly across top of Panel Pat. Pat to end of row.

Bind off 8 {**9**-10-**11**-11-**12**-13-**14**} sts beg next row.

Bind off 4 sts beg next row.

Bind off rem 7 {**9**-10-**10**-12-**13**-13-**14**} sts.

FRONT

Work as for Back until 10 {**10**-10-**12**-12-**12**-12-**12**} rows less than Back have been worked to beg of shoulder shaping, thus ending with right side facing for next row.

Shape neck: Next row: (Right Side). Pat 31 {**35**-38-**40**-42-**45**-47-**50**} sts. Turn and work this side first.

Bind off 4 {**4**-4-**3**-3-**3**-3-**3**} sts at beg of next row. 27 {**31**-34-**37**-39-**42**-44-**47**} sts.

Dec 1 st at neck edge on next 2 rows, then on following alt rows 2 {**2**-2-**3**-3-**3**-3-**3**} times. 23 {**27**-30-**32**-34-**37**-39-**42**} sts.

Work 2 rows even in pat, thus ending with right side facing for next row.

Shape shoulder: Bind off 8 {**9**-10-**11**-11-**12**-13-**14**} sts beg of next and following alt row.

Work 1 row even.

Bind off rem 7 {**9**-10-**10**-12-**13**-13-**14**} sts.

With right side facing, rejoin yarn to rem sts. Bind off center 15 {**15**-17-**18**-20-**20**-22-**22**} sts, dec 4 sts evenly across top of Panel Pat. Pat to end of row. 31 {**35**-38-**40**-42-**45**-47-**50**} sts.

Work 1 row even.

Bind off 4 {**4**-4-**3**-3-**3**-3-**3**} sts at beg of next row. 27 {**31**-34-**37**-39-**42**-44-**47**} sts.

Dec 1 st at neck edge on next 2 rows, then on following alt rows 2 {**2**-2-**3**-3-**3**-3-**3**} times. 23 {**27**-30-**32**-34-**37**-39-**42**} sts.

Work 2 rows even in pat, thus ending with **wrong side** facing for next row.

5

Shape shoulder: Bind off 8 {**9**-10-**11**-11-**12**-13-**14**} sts beg of next and following alt row.
Work 1 row even.
Bind off rem 7 {**9**-10-**10**-12-**13**-13-**14**} sts.

SLEEVES

With smaller needles, cast on 41 {**47**-51-**55**-59-**59**-61-**61**} sts.
Work 4 rows in garter st, ending with right side facing for next row.

Change to larger needles and proceed in pat as follows:

1st row: (Right Side). Inc 1 st in first st. P19 {**22**-24-**26**-28-**28**-29-**29**}. MB. P19 {**22**-24-**26**-28-**28**-29-**29**}. Inc 1 st in last st. 43 {**49**-53-**57**-61-**61**-63-**63**} sts.

2nd and every following alt row: Knit.

3rd row: P20 {**23**-25-**27**-29-**29**-30-**30**}. MB. P1. MB. P20 {**23**-25-**27**-29-**29**-30-**30**}.

5th row: Inc 1 st in first st. P20 {**23**-25-**27**-29-**29**-30-**30**}. MB. P20 {**23**-25-**27**-29-**29**-30-**30**}. Inc 1 st in last st. 45 {**51**-55-**59**-63-**63**-65-**65**} sts.

7th row: Purl.

9th row: Inc 1 st in first st. P5 {**8**-10-**12**-14-**14**-15-**15**}. MB. P31. MB. P5 {**8**-10-**12**-14-**14**-15-**15**}. Inc 1 st in last st. 47 {**53**-57-**61**-65-**65**-67-**67**} sts.

11th row: P6 {**9**-11-**13**-15-**15**-16-**16**}. MB. P1. MB. P29. MB. P1. MB. P6 {**9**-11-**13**-15-**15**-16-**16**}.

13th row: Inc 1 st in first st. P6 {**9**-11-**13**-15-**15**-16-**16**}. MB. P31. MB. P6 {**9**-11-**13**-15-**15**-16-**16**}. Inc 1 st in last st. 49 {**55**-59-**63**-67-**67**-69-**69**} sts.

15th row: Purl.

17th row: (Inc 1 st in first st) 1 {**1**-1-**1**-0-**0**-1-**1**} time. P47 {**53**-57-**61**-1-**1**-1-**1**}. (MB. P63. MB. P1) 0 {**0**-0-**0**-1-**1**-1-**1**} time. (Inc 1 st in last st) 1 {**1**-1-**1**-0-**0**-1-**1**} time. 51 {**57**-61-**65**-67-**67**-71-**71**} sts.

19th row: (Inc 1 st in first st) 0 {**0**-0-**0**-1-**1**-0-**0**} time. P51 {**57**-61-**65**-1-**1**-2-**2**}. (MB. P61. MB. P1) 0 {**0**-0-**0**-1-**1**-0-**0**} time. (MB. P1. MB. P61. MB. P1. MB. P2) 0 {**0**-0-**0**-0-**0**-1-**1**} time. (Inc 1 st in last st) 0 {**0**-0-**0**-1-**1**-0-**0**} time. 51 {**57**-61-**65**-69-**69**-71-**71**} sts.

21st row: (Inc 1 st in first st) 1 {**1**-1-**1**-0-**0**-1-**1**} time. P49 {**55**-59-**63**-2-**2**-2-**2**}. (MB. P63. MB. P2) 0 {**0**-0-**0**-1-**1**-1-**1**} time. (Inc 1 st in last st) 1 {**1**-1-**1**-0-**0**-1-**1**} time. 53 {**59**-63-**67**-69-**69**-73-**73**} sts.

23rd row: Purl.

24th row: Knit.

These 24 rows form Bobble Pat and beg sleeve shaping.

Cont in pat, shaping sides by inc 1 st at each end of every following 4th row from previous inc until there are 81 {**69**-75-**75**-99-**99**-103-**103**} sts, taking inc sts into pat.

Sizes 8, 10 and Extra-Small only: Inc 1 st at each end of every following 6th row until there are {**83**-91-**95**} sts, taking inc sts into pat.

All Sizes: Cont even in pat until Sleeve from beg measures 12½ {**14¼**-16-**17½**-18¼-**18¾**-19-**19**}", ending with right side facing for next row.
Bind off in pat.
Place markers along side edges of Sleeves 1 {**1**-1-**1¼**-1¼-**1¼**-1¼-**1¼**}" down from bound off edge.

FINISHING

Pin garment pieces to measurements. Cover with a damp cloth leaving to dry.
Join right shoulder seam.

Neckband: With right side of work facing and smaller needles, pick up and knit 14 {**14**-14-**16**-16-**16**-16-**16**} sts down Left Front neck edge, 11 {**11**-13-**14**-16-**16**-18-**18**} sts across center Front, 14 {**14**-14-**16**-16-**16**-16-**16**} sts up Right Front neck edge and 27 {**27**-29-**30**-32-**32**-34-**34**} sts around Back neck edge. 66 {**66**-70-**76**-80-**80**-84-**84**} sts.
Work in garter st for 2 rows, ending with **wrong side** facing for next row. Bind off knitwise (**wrong side**).

Sew left shoulder and neckband seam. Sew side seams. Sew in sleeves placing rows above markers along bound off sts of Front and Back to form square armholes.

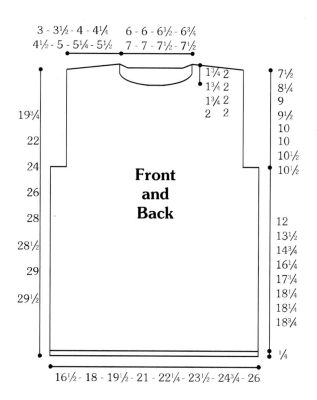

3 - 3½ - 4 - 4¼   6 - 6 - 6½ - 6¾
4½ - 5 - 5¼ - 5½   7 - 7 - 7½ - 7½

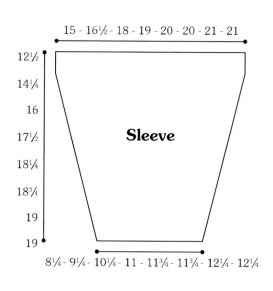

15 - 16½ - 18 - 19 - 20 - 20 - 21 - 21

19¾
22
24
26
28
28½
29
29½

**Front
and
Back**

1¾ 2   7½
1¾ 2   8¼
1¾ 2   9
2   2   9½
        10
        10
        10½
        10½

12
13½
14¾
16¼
17¾
18¼
18¼
18¾

¼

16½ - 18 - 19½ - 21 - 22¼ - 23½ - 24¾ - 26

12½
14¼
16
17½
18¼
18¾
19
19

Sleeve

8¼ - 9¼ - 10¼ - 11 - 11¾ - 11¾ - 12¼ - 12¼

Panel Pat A

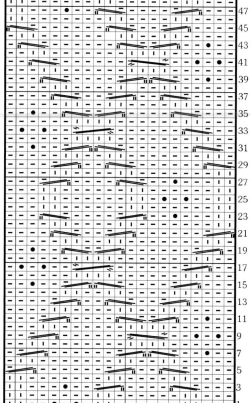

Start Here

Panel Pat B

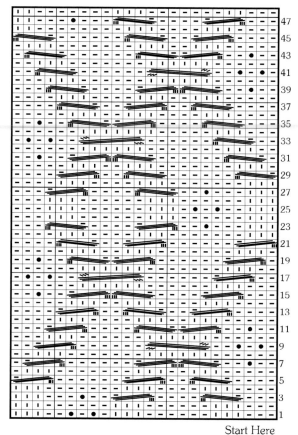

Start Here

Key for Panel Pat A

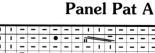

| = Knit on Right Side, purl on Wrong Side

— = Purl on Right Side, knit on Wrong Side

● = MB

= Cr3L

= Cr3R

= C4B

Key for Panel Pat B

| = Knit on Right Side, purl on Wrong Side

— = Purl on Right Side, knit on Wrong Side

● = MB

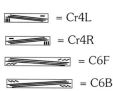

= Cr4L

= Cr4R

= C6F

= C6B

7

2. Nautical Options

SIZES

Chest/bust measurement

6	25"
8	26½"
10	28"
Extra-Small	32"
Small	34"
Medium	36"
Large	38"
Extra-Large	40"

Finished chest/bust

6	30½"
8	33"
10	34½"
Extra-Small	37"
Small	38½"
Medium	41"
Large	42½"
Extra-Large	45"

Size Note: *Instructions are written for size 6, with sizes 8, 10, Extra-Small, Small, Medium, Large, and Extra-Large in braces { }. Instructions will be easier to read if you circle all the numbers pertaining to your size. If only one number is given, it applies to all sizes.*

MATERIALS

Worsted Weight Yarn: 3½ oz (223 yds/100 g)

Sizes	6	8	10	XS	S	M	L	XL	
Long Sleeve Pullover									
Red	**2**	**3**	**3**	**4**	**4**	**4**	**5**	**5**	balls
White	**1**	**1**	**1**	**1**	**2**	**2**	**2**	**2**	ball(s)
Sleeveless Pullover									
Red	**3**	**3**	**3**	**4**	**4**	**4**	**4**	**5**	balls

Samples made with **Patons Classic Merino Wool.**

Sizes 6 (4 mm) and 7 (4.5 mm) knitting needles **or size needed for gauge.**

GAUGE SWATCH

20 sts and 26 rows = 4" with larger needles in stocking st.

STITCH GUIDE

M1P = make one st by picking up horizontal loop lying before next st and purling into back of loop.

LONG SLEEVE SWEATER

BACK
With smaller needles and Red, cast on 74 {81**-88-**95**-95-**102**-109-**109**} sts.
1st row: (Right Side). K4. *P3. K4. Rep from * to end of row.
2nd row: P4. *K3. P4. Rep from * to end of row. These 2 rows form rib pat.
Work a further 9 {**9**-11-**11**-13-**14**-13-**13**} rows in rib pat.

Sizes 6, 8, S, and XL only: Next row: (Wrong Side). Rib, inc 2 {**1**-1-**3**} st(s) evenly across. 76 {**82**-96-**112**} sts.

Sizes 10, XS and L only: Next row: (Wrong Side). Rib, dec {2-**3**-3} sts evenly across. {86-**92**-106} sts.

All Sizes: Change to larger needles and proceed in stripe pat as follows:
With White, work 2 rows stocking st.
With Red, work 6 rows stocking st.
These 8 rows form stripe pat.

Cont in stripe pat until Back from beg measures 9 {**10¼**-11½-**11¾**-12¼-**12¼**-12½-**12½**}", ending with right side facing for next row.**

Shape armholes: Keeping cont of stripe pat, bind off 4 {**4**-5-**5**-6-**6**-7-**7**} sts beg next 2 rows. 68 {**74**-76-**82**-84-**90**-92-**98**} sts.
Dec 1 st each end of next 3 {**5**-5-**7**-7-**9**-9-**11**} rows, then on following alt rows twice. 58 {**60**-62-**64**-66-**68**-70-**72**} sts.

Cont even in pat until armhole measures 6¾ {**7**-7½-**8**-8-**8**-8¼-**8¾**}", ending with right side facing for next row.

Shape shoulders and back neck: Bind off 5 sts beg next 2 rows. 48 {**50**-52-**54**-56-**58**-60-**62**} sts.
Next row: (Right Side). Bind off 5 sts. Knit across until there are 7 {**7**-7-**7**-8-**9**-9-**10**} sts on right-hand needle. Turn and work this side first.
Bind off 3 {**3**-3-**3**-4-**4**-4-**4**} sts beg next row.
Bind off rem 4 {**4**-4-**4**-4-**5**-5-**6**} sts.

With right side facing, rejoin yarn to rem sts. Bind off center 24 {**26**-28-**30**-30-**30**-32-**32**} sts. Knit to end of row.
Bind off 5 sts beg next row.
Bind off 3 {**3**-3-**3**-4-**4**-4-**4**} sts beg next row.
Bind off rem 4 {**4**-4-**4**-4-**5**-5-**6**} sts.

FRONT
Work as for Back until 12 rows less than Back have been worked to beg of shoulder shaping, thus ending with right side facing for next row.

Shape neck: Next row: (Right Side). K21 {**21**-21-**21**-22-**23**-23-**24**}. Turn and work this side first.
Bind off 3 {**3**-3-**3**-4-**4**-4-**4**} sts beg next row. 18 {**18**-18-**18**-18-**19**-19-**20**} sts.
Dec 1 st at neck edge on next 2 rows, then on following alt rows twice. 14 {**14**-14-**14**-14-**15**-15-**16**} sts.
Work 4 rows even, thus ending with right side facing for next row.

Shape shoulder: Bind off 5 sts beg next and following alt row.
Work 1 row even.
Bind off rem 4 {**4**-4-**4**-4-**5**-5-**6**} sts.

With right side facing, rejoin yarn to rem sts. Bind off center 16 {**18**-20-**22**-22-**22**-24-**24**} sts. Knit to end of row.
Work 1 row even.
Bind off 3 {**3**-3-**3**-4-**4**-4-**4**} sts beg next row. 18 {**18**-18-**18**-18-**19**-19-**20**} sts.
Dec 1 st at neck edge on next 2 rows, then on following alt rows twice. 14 {**14**-14-**14**-14-**15**-15-**16**} sts.
Work 4 rows even, thus ending with **wrong side** facing for next row.

Shape shoulder: Bind off 5 sts beg next and following alt row.
Work 1 row even.
Bind off rem 4 {**4**-4-**4**-4-**5**-5-**6**} sts.

SLEEVES
With smaller needles and Red, cast on 39 {**39**-39-**46**-46-**46**-46-**46**} sts.
Work 11 {**11**-13-**13**-16-**16**-15-**15**} rows in rib pat as given for Back.

Sizes 6 and XS only: Next row: (Wrong Side). Rib, dec 1 {**2**} st(s) evenly across. 38 {**44**} sts.

Sizes 8, 10, L and XL only: Next row: (Wrong Side). Rib, inc {**1**-3-**2**-2} st(s) evenly across. {**40**-42-48-**48**} sts.

All Sizes: Change to larger needles and proceed as follows:
Beg with 6 rows of Red, proceed in stripe pat, shaping sides by inc 1 st at each end of next and every following 6th {**6th**-8th-**8th**-8th-**6th**-6th-**6th**} row to 48 {**48**-62-**62**-66-**52**-54-**62**} sts, then on every following 8th {**8th**-10th-**10th**-10th-**8th**-8th-**8th**} row until there are 58 {**62**-64-**66**-68-**70**-72-**74**} sts. Cont even in stripe pat until Sleeve from beg measures 14 {**15½**-17-**18**-18½-**18½**-19-**19**}", ending with right side facing for next row.

Shape top: Keeping cont of stripe pat, bind off 3 {**3**-3-**3**-4-**4**-4-**4**} sts beg next 2 rows. 52 {**56**-58-**60**-60-**62**-64-**66**} sts.

Dec 1 st each end of next and following alt rows until there are 32 {**36**-36-**36**-36-**36**-36-**40**} sts, then on every row until there are 24 sts.
Bind off 3 sts beg next 4 rows.
Bind off rem 12 sts.

FINISHING

Pin garment pieces to measurements. Cover with a damp cloth leaving to dry.
Join right shoulder seam.

Neckband: With right side of work facing, smaller needles and Red, pick up and knit 14 {**15**-14-**15**-15-**15**-15-**15**} sts down Left Front neck edge, 16 {**18**-20-**22**-22-**22**-24-**24**} sts across center Front, 14 {**15**-14-**15**-15-**15**-15-**15**} sts up Right Front neck edge and 30 {**33**-33-**36**-36-**36**-41-**41**} sts across Back neck edge. 74 {**81**-81-**88**-88-**88**-95-**95**} sts.
1st row: (Wrong Side). P4. *K3. P4. Rep from * to end of row.
2nd row: K4. *P3. K4. Rep from * to end of row.
Rep last 2 rows 5 {**5**-6-**6**-7-**7**-7-**7**} times more.
Bind off loosely in ribbing.

Sew left shoulder and neckband seam. Sew side and sleeve seams. Sew in sleeves.

SLEEVELESS TOP
BACK

Work from ** to ** as given for Back of Long Sleeve Pullover omitting all reference to stripe pat.

Shape armholes: Bind off 6 {**6**-7-**7**-8-**8**-9-**9**} sts beg next 2 rows. 64 {**70**-72-**78**-80-**86**-88-**94**} sts.
Dec 1 st each end of next 3 rows, then on following alt rows 1 {**3**-3-**5**-5-**7**-7-**9**} time(s), then on every following 4th row until 52 {**54**-56-**58**-60-**62**-64-**66**} sts rem.

Cont even until armhole measures 6¾ {**7**-7½-**8**-8-**8¼**-8¼-**8¾**}", ending with right side facing for next row.

Shape shoulders and back neck: Next row: (Right Side). Bind off 5 {**5**-5-**5**-5-**6**-6-**6**} sts. Knit across until there are 9 {**9**-9-**9**-10-**10**-10-**11**} sts on right-hand needle. Turn and work this side first.
Bind off 3 {**3**-3-**3**-4-**4**-4-**4**} sts beg next row.
Bind off rem 6 {**6**-6-**6**-6-**6**-6-**7**} sts.

With right side facing, rejoin yarn to rem sts. Bind off center 24 {**26**-28-**30**-30-**30**-32-**32**} sts. Knit to end of row.
Bind off 5 {**5**-5-**5**-5-**6**-6-**6**} sts. Purl to end of row.
Bind off 3 {**3**-3-**3**-4-**4**-4-**4**} sts beg next row.
Bind off rem 6 {**6**-6-**6**-6-**6**-6-**7**} sts.

FRONT

Work as for Back until 12 rows less than Back have been worked to beg of shoulder shaping, thus ending with right side facing for next row.

Shape neck: Next row: (Right Side). K18 {**18**-18-**18**-19-**20**-20-**21**}. Turn and work this side first.
Bind off 3 {**3**-3-**3**-4-**4**-4-**4**} sts beg next row. 15 {**15**-15-**15**-15-**16**-16-**17**} sts.
Dec 1 st at neck edge on next 2 rows, then on following alt rows twice. 11 {**11**-11-**11**-11-**12**-12-**13**} sts.
Work 4 rows even, thus ending with right side facing for next row.

Shape shoulder: Bind off 5 {**5**-5-**5**-5-**6**-6-**6**} sts beg next row.
Work 1 row even.
Bind off rem 6 {**6**-6-**6**-6-**6**-6-**7**} sts.

With right side facing, rejoin yarn to rem sts. Bind off center 16 {**18**-20-**22**-22-**22**-24-**24**} sts. Knit to end of row.
Work 1 row even.
Bind off 3 {**3**-3-**3**-4-**4**-4-**4**} sts beg next row. 15 {**15**-15-**15**-15-**16**-16-**17**} sts.
Dec 1 st at neck edge on next 2 rows, then on following alt rows twice. 11 {**11**-11-**11**-11-**12**-12-**13**} sts.
Work 4 rows even, thus ending with **wrong side** facing for next row.

Shape shoulder: Bind off 5 {**5**-5-**5**-5-**6**-6-**6**} sts beg next row.
Work 1 row even.
Bind off rem 6 {**6**-6-**6**-6-**6**-6-**7**} sts.

Pin garment pieces to measurements. Cover with a damp cloth leaving to dry.
Sew right shoulder seam.

Collar: With right side of work facing and smaller needles, pick up and knit 16 {**17**-16-**17**-17-**17**-17-**17**} sts down Left Front neck edge, 17 {**19**-21-**23**-

23-**23**-25-**25**} sts across center Front, 16 {**17**-16-**17**-17-**17**-17-**17**} sts up Right Front neck edge and 30 {**33**-33-**36**-36-**36**-41-**41**} sts across Back neck edge. 79 {**86**-86-**93**-93-**93**-100-**100**} sts.

1st row: (Wrong Side). K3. *P3. K4. Rep from * to last 6 sts. P3. K3.

2nd row: P3. *K3. P4. Rep from * to last 6 sts. K3. P3.

Rep these 2 rows for 3 {**3**-3½-**3½**-4-**4**-4-**4**}", ending with **wrong side** facing for next row.

Change to larger needles.

Next row: K3. *P2. M1P. P1. K4. Rep from * to last 6 sts. P2. M1P. P1. K3. 90 {**98**-98-**106**-106-**106**-114-**114**} sts.

Next row: P3. *K4. P4. Rep from * to last 7 sts. K4. P3.

Next row: K3. *P4. K4. Rep from * to last 7 sts. P4. K3.

Rep last 2 rows until Collar measures 8 {**8**-8¾-**9½**-10¼-**10¼**-10¼-**10¼**}".

Bind off in ribbing.

Sew left shoulder and Collar seam, reversing Collar seam for turn-back.

Armbands: With RS of work facing and smaller needles, pick up and knit 76 {**80**-86-**90**-92-**96**-98-**102**} sts evenly around armhole edge.

Knit 2 rows. Bind off knitwise (**wrong side**). Sew side and armband seams.

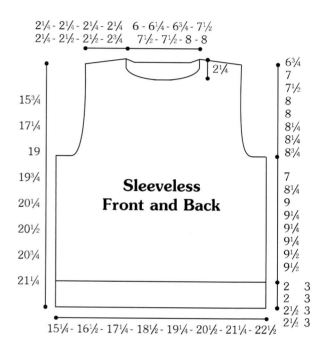

Sleeveless Front and Back

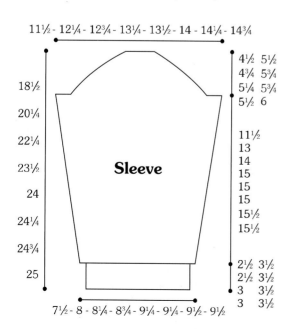

Sleeve

Long Sleeve Front and Back

3. Cabled Tunic & Sailor Dress   Intermediate

SIZES

Tunic
To fit bust measurement

Small	32"
Medium	34"
Large	36"
Extra-Large	38"

Finished bust measurement

Small	37"
Medium	40"
Large	42"
Extra-Large	45"

Dress
Chest measurement

12 mos	18"
18 mos	19"
2 yrs	21"

Finished chest

12 mos	22"
18 mos	24"
2 yrs	26"

Size Note: Instructions for Cabled Tunic are written for size Small, with sizes Medium, Large, and Extra-Large in braces { }. Instructions for Sailor Dress are written for size 12 mos, with sizes 18 mos and 2 yrs in braces { }. Instructions will be easier to read if you circle all the numbers pertaining to your size. If only one number is given, it applies to all sizes.

MATERIALS

Tunic
Sport Weight Yarn: 1¾ oz (136 yds/50 g)

Sizes	S	M	L	XL	
White	16	16	17	18	balls
Blue	1	1	1	1	ball

Sample made with **Patons Grace**.

Sizes 3 (3.25 mm) and 5 (3.75 mm) knitting needles **or size needed for gauge**. Cable needle. 3 st holders.

Dress
Sport Weight Yarn:
1¾ oz (136 yds/50 g)

Sizes	12 mos	18 mos	2 yrs	
White	6	7	8	balls
Blue	1	1	1	ball

Sample made with **Patons Grace**.

Sizes 3 (3.25 mm) and 5 (3.75 mm) knitting needles. Pair of size 5 (3.75 mm) double-pointed needles **or size needed for gauge**. Cable needle. 3 stitch holders.

GAUGE SWATCH

Tunic
32 sts and 38 rows = 4" with larger needles in Cable Pat.

Dress
30 sts and 38 rows = 4" with larger needles in Panel Pat.

STITCH GUIDE

C5F = slip next 3 sts onto a cable needle and leave at front of work. K2, then K3 from cable needle.

C5B = slip next 2 sts onto a cable needle and leave at back of work. K3, then K2 from cable needle.

TUNIC

Cable Pat (worked over 10 sts).
1st row: (Right Side). P3. C5B. K2.
2nd and alt rows: Purl.
3rd and 7th rows: P3. K7.
5th row: P3. K2. C5F.
8th row: Purl.
These 8 rows form Cable Pat.

BACK

With smaller needles and White, cast on 121 {131**-137-**147**} sts.
1st row: (Right Side). K3 {**0**-3-**0**}. *P3. K5. Rep from * to last 6 {**3**-6-**3**} sts. P3. K3 {**0**-3-**0**}.
2nd row: Purl.
Rep last 2 rows 3 times more, then 1st row once.
With Blue, beg with purl row, rep last 2 rows once. Break Blue.
With White, beg with purl row, rep last 2 rows until work from beg measures 3½", ending with right side facing for next row.

Change to larger needles and proceed in Cable Pat as follows:
1st row: (Right Side). K3 {**0**-3-**0**}. *P3. Inc 1 st in next st. K3. Inc 1 st in next st. Rep from * to last 6 {**3**-6-**3**} sts. P3. K3 {**0**-3-**0**}. 149 {**163**-169-**183**} sts.
2nd row: Purl.
3rd row: K3 {**0**-3-**0**}. (Work 1st row of Cable Pat) 14 {**16**-16-**18**} times. P3. K3 {**0**-3-**0**}.
4th row: Purl.
5th row: K3 {**0**-3-**0**}. (Work 3rd row of Cable Pat) 14 {**16**-16-**18**} times. P3. K3 {**0**-3-**0**}.
6th row: As 4th row.
Cable Pat is now in position.
Cont in pat until work from beg measures 16 {**16½**-16½-**16¾**}", ending with right side facing for next row.

Proceed in rib pat as follows:
1st row: (Right Side). K3 {**0**-3-**0**}. *P3. Sl1. K1. psso. K3. K2tog. Rep from * to last 6 {**3**-6-**3**} sts. P3. K3 {**0**-3-**0**}. 121 {**131**-137-**147**} sts.

2nd row: Purl.
3rd row: K3 {**0**-3-**0**}. *P3. K5. Rep from * to last 6 {**3**-6-**3**} sts. P3. K3 {**0**-3-**0**}.
4th row: Purl.
Rep last 2 rows until work from beg measures 17 {**17½**-17½-**17¾**}", ending with right side facing for next row.

Armhole shaping: Bind off 11 {**8**-11-**8**} sts beg next 2 rows. 99 {**115**-115-**131**} sts.**

Cont even in pat until armhole measures 7½ {**7½**-8-**8½**}", ending with right side facing for next row.

Shoulder shaping: Keeping cont of pat, bind off 28 {**36**-36-**43**} sts beg next 2 rows. Leave rem 43 {**43**-43-**45**} sts on a st holder.

FRONT

Work from ** to ** as given for Back.
Cont even in pat until armhole measures 1½ {**1½**-2-**2¼**}", ending with right side facing for next row.

Neck opening: Next row: Pat across 48 {**56**-56-**64**} sts. **Turn.** Leave rem sts on a spare needle.
Next row: (**Wrong Side**). Cast on 3 sts. Knit these 3 sts. Pat to end of row. 51 {**59**-59-**67**} sts.
Next row: Pat to last 3 sts. K3.

Cont in pat, keeping 3 sts at neck opening in garter st, until armhole measures 4½ {**4½**-4½-**5**}", ending with right side facing for next row.

Neck shaping: Pat to last 13 {**13**-13-**14**} sts. **Turn.** Leave these 13 {**13**-13-**14**} sts on a st holder.
Dec 1 st at neck edge on next 10 rows. 28 {**36**-36-**43**} sts.

Cont even in pat until work from beg measures same length as Back to shoulder, ending with right side facing for next row. Bind off.

With right side of work facing, rejoin White to rem 51 {**59**-59-**67**} sts. K3. Pat to end of row.
Next row: Pat to last 3 sts. K3.

Cont in pat, keeping 3 sts at neck opening in garter st, until armhole measures 4½ {**4½**-4½-**5**}", ending with right side facing for next row.

17

Slip first 13 {13-13-14} sts onto a st holder. Join yarn to rem sts and pat to end of row.

Dec 1 st at neck edge on next 10 rows. 28 {36-36-43} sts.

Cont even in pat until work from beg measures same length as Back to shoulder, ending with right side facing for next row. Bind off.

SLEEVES

With smaller needles and White, cast on 59 {67-67-75} sts.

1st row: (Right Side). Purl.
2nd row: P3. *K5. P3. Rep from * to end of row.
Rep last 2 rows 3 times more, then 1st row once.
With Blue, rep last 2 rows once. Break Blue.
With White, rep last 2 rows until work from beg measures 7", ending with a 1st row. Place markers 3½" above cast on edge for turn-back.

Change to larger needles and, reversing **wrong side** to right side, proceed as follows:

1st row: (Right Side). *P3. Inc 1 st in next st. K3. Inc 1 st in next st. Rep from * to last 3 sts. P3. 73 {83-83-93} sts.
2nd row: Purl.
3rd row: (Work 1st row of Cable Pat) 7 {8-8-9} times. P3.
4th row: Purl.
Cable Pat is now in position.

Cont in Cable Pat, at the same time, inc 1 st each end of needle on next and every following 4th row to 119 {119-129-135} sts, taking inc sts into pat.

Cont even in pat until work from beg measures 22½ {23½-23½-24½}", ending with right side facing for next row. Bind off in pat.

FINISHING

Pin garment pieces to measurements. Cover with a damp cloth leaving to dry.

Collar: Sew shoulder seams. With right side of work facing, smaller needles and White, P13 {13-13-14} from Right Front st holder. Pick up and purl 19 sts up Right Front neck edge. P43 {43-43-45} from Back st holder, dec 0 {0-0-4} sts evenly across. Pick up and purl 19 sts down Left Front neck edge. P13 {13-13-14} from Left Front st holder. 107 sts.

1st row: (Wrong Side). P3. *K5. P3. Rep from * to end of row.
2nd row: Purl.
Rep last 2 rows until Collar measures 4", ending with a 1st row. Change to Blue and beg with a purl row, cont in ribbing for 2 rows. Change to White and beg with a purl row, cont in ribbing for 6 rows. Bind off in ribbing.

With **wrong side** facing, sew 3 cast on sts at Left neck opening in position to wrong side. Place markers 1¾ {1¼-1¾-1¼}" down from bound off edge at each side of sleeve. Sew in sleeves, placing rows above markers between bound off sts at Front and Back armholes to form square armholes. Sew side and sleeve seams, reversing seam for cuff turn-back.

DRESS

STITCH GUIDE

C4F = slip next 2 sts onto a cable needle and leave at front of work. K2, then K3 from cable needle.
C4B = slip next 2 sts onto a cable needle and leave at back of work. K2, then K2 from cable needle.
Sl1K = slip next st knitwise.

Panel Pat (worked over 8 sts).
1st row: (Right Side). P2. C4B. K2.
2nd and alt rows: Purl.
3rd row: P2. K6.
5th row: P2. K2. C4F.
7th row: As 3rd row.
8th row: Purl.
These 8 rows form Panel Pat.

BACK

**With smaller needles and White, cast on 192 {216-240} sts.

1st row: (Right Side). K7. *Sl1K. K7. P1. K15. Rep from * to last 17 sts. Sl1K. K7. P1. K8.
2nd row: P8. *K1. P7. K1. P15. Rep from * to last 16 sts. (K1. P7) twice.

Change to larger needles and rep last 2 rows until work from beg measures 6 {7-7½}", ending with right side facing for next row.

Next row: (Right Side). (Make Pleats). *Slip 8 sts onto 1st double-pointed needle. Slip next 8 sts onto 2nd double-pointed needle. Turn 2nd needle (**wrong side** of both needles face each other). Align left-hand needle behind the two double-pointed needles and knit tog one st from each of 3 needles (3 sets of 8 sts will be worked tog) - Pleat made. Rep from * to end of row. 64 {**72**-80} sts.
Next row: Purl, dec 2 {inc 0-inc 2} sts evenly across. 62 {**72**-82} sts.
Next 2 rows: With Blue, knit.
Next 2 rows: With White, knit.
Next 2 rows: With Blue, knit.
Next row: With White, knit.
Next row: Purl.

Proceed in Panel Pat as follows:
1st row: (Right Side). *P2 {**3**-4}. Inc 1 st in next st. K2 {**3**-4}. Inc 1 st in next st. Rep from * to last 2 {**0**-2} sts. P2 {**0**-2}. 82 {**90**-98} sts.
2nd row: Purl.
3rd row: (Work 1st row of Panel Pat) 10 {**11**-12} times. P2.
4th row: Purl.
Panel Pat is now in position.
Cont in pat until work from beg measures 12½ {**14**-15}", ending with right side facing for next row.

Armhole shaping: Keeping cont of pat, bind off 3 sts beg next 2 rows. 76 {**84**-92} sts. Dec 1 st each end of needle on next 3 rows, then on following alt rows twice. 66 {**74**-82} sts.**

Cont even in pat until armhole measures 4½ {**5**-5½}", ending with right side facing for next row.

Back neck shaping: Next row: Pat 20 {**22**-26} sts. Turn. Leave rem sts on a st holder.
Dec 1 st at neck edge on next 3 rows. Bind off rem 17 {**19**-23} sts.

With right side of work facing, join White to rem sts and bind off next 26 {**30**-30} sts. Pat to end of row. Dec 1 st at neck edge on next 3 rows.
Bind off rem 17 {**19**-23} sts.

FRONT
Work from ** to ** as given for Back.
Cont even in pat until armhole measures 1½", ending with right side facing for next row.

V-Neck shaping: Next row: Pat 31 {**35**-39} sts. **Turn.** Leave rem sts on a spare needle.
Dec 1 st at V-neck edge on next 3 {**3**-1} row(s), then every alt row to 17 {**19**-23} sts.

Cont even in pat until armhole measures same length as Back to shoulder, ending with right side facing for next row. Bind off.

With right side of work facing, join White to rem sts. Bind off center 4 sts. Pat to end of row.
Dec 1 st at V-neck edge on next 3 {**3**-1} row(s), then every alt row to 17 {**19**-23} sts.

Cont even in pat until armhole measures same length as Back to shoulder, ending with **wrong side** facing for next row. Bind off.

SLEEVES
With smaller needles and Blue, cast on 44 {**50**-56} sts.
Next row: (**Wrong Side**). With Blue, knit.
Next 2 rows: With White, knit.
Next 2 rows: With Blue, knit.
Change to larger needles and White, proceed as follows:
1st row: (Right Side). *K2. Inc 1 st in next st. K2. Inc 1 st in next st. Rep from * to last 2 sts. K2. 58 {**66**-74} sts.
2nd row: Purl.
3rd row: (Work 1st row of Panel Pat) 7 {**8**-9} times. P2.
4th row: Purl.
5th row: (Work 3rd row of Panel Pat) 7 {**8**-9} times. P2.
6th row: As 4th row.
Panel Pat is now in position.
Cont in pat, keeping cont of Panel Pat, inc 1 st each end of needle on next and following 4th row, taking inc sts into garter st. Work 1 row even, thus ending with right side facing for next row. 62 {**70**-78} sts.

Cap shaping: Keep cont of pat, bind off 2 sts beg next 2 rows. Dec 1 st each end of needle on next 12 {**14**-16} rows. Bind off 2 sts beg next 6 rows. Bind off rem 22 {**26**-30} sts.

FINISHING
Pin garment pieces to measurements. Cover with a damp cloth leaving to dry.

Sailor Collar

With smaller needles and Blue, cast on 60 {**66**-72} sts.

1st row: (**Wrong Side**). With Blue, knit.
2nd row: With White, Sl1K. K1. psso. Knit to last 2 sts. K2tog.
3rd row: With White, knit.
4th row: With Blue, Sl1K. K1. psso. Knit to last 2 sts. K2tog.
5th row: With Blue, knit.
6th row: With White, Sl1K. K1. psso. Knit to last 2 sts. K2tog. 54 {**60**-66} sts. Place markers at each end of row.

Change to larger needles and White. Beg with a purl row, proceed in stocking st until work from beg measures 4½ {**5**-5}", ending with right side facing for next row.
Next row: K12 {**13**-16}. K2tog. **Turn.** Leave rem sts on a st holder.
Next row: P2tog. Purl to end of row.
Next row: Knit to last 2 sts. K2tog.
Next row: Cast on 3 sts. Purl to end of row. 14 {**15**-18} sts.

Tie shaping: 1st row: (Right Side). K1. Sl1K. K1. psso. Knit to end of row.
2nd row: Purl to last 3 sts. P2togtbl. P1.
3rd row: K1. Sl1K. K1. psso. Knit to last 2 sts. Inc 1 st in next st. K1.
4th row: As 2nd row.
Rep last 4 rows 0 {**1**-1} time more. 11 {**9**-12} sts.

Proceed as follows:
1st row: (Right Side). K1. Sl1K. K1. psso. Knit to end of row.
2nd row: Purl.
3rd row: K1. Sl1K. K1. psso. Knit to last 2 sts. Inc 1 st in next st. K1.
4th row: Purl.
Rep last 4 rows 5 {**5**-6} times more. 5 {**3**-5} sts.
Work 4 rows even in stocking st. Bind off (right side).

With right side of work facing, join yarn to rem sts. Bind off 26 {**30**-30} sts. Knit to end of row.
Dec 1 st at neck edge on next 3 rows. 11 {**12**-15} sts.
Next row: Cast on 3 sts. Knit to end of row. 14 {**15**-18} sts.
Next row: Purl.

Tie shaping: 1st row: (Right Side). Knit to last 3 sts. K2tog. K1.
2nd row: P1. P2tog. Purl to end of row.
3rd row: Inc 1 st in first st. Knit to last 3 sts. K2tog. K1.
4th row: As 2nd row.
Rep last 4 rows 0 {**1**-1} time more. 11 {**9**-12} sts.

Proceed as follows:
1st row: (Right Side). Knit to last 3 sts. K2tog. K1.
2nd row: Purl.
3rd row: Inc 1 st in first st. Knit to last 3 sts. K2tog. K1.
4th row: Purl.
Rep last 4 rows 5 {**5**-6} times more. 5 {**3**-5} sts.
Work 4 rows even in stocking st. Bind off (right side).

Right side edge of Collar: With right side of work facing, smaller needles and Blue, pick up and knit 58 {**61**-64} sts from marker along right edge of Collar.
Next row: (**Wrong Side**). Cast on 15 sts. Knit to last 2 sts. Inc 1 st in next st. K1.
Next row: With White, inc 1 st in first st. Knit to end of row.
Next row: With White, knit.
Next row: With Blue, inc 1 st in first st. Knit to end of row.
Next row: With Blue, knit. Bind off knitwise (right side).

Left side edge of Collar: With right side of work facing, smaller needles and Blue, pick up and knit 58 {**61**-64} sts along left edge of Collar to marker.
Next row: (**Wrong Side**). Inc 1 st in first st. Knit to end of row. Turn. Cast on 15 sts.
Next row: With White, knit.
Next row: With White, inc 1 st in first st. Knit to end of row.
Next row: With Blue, knit.
Next row: With Blue, inc 1 st in first st. Knit to end of row.
Bind off knitwise (right side).

Ring: With White and smaller needles, cast on 3 sts. Proceed in stocking st for 2". Bind off. Sew cast on and bound off edges tog to form a ring.

Inset: With White, cast on 5 sts.
1st row: (Right Side). With White, inc 1 st in first st. Knit to last 2 sts. Inc 1 st in next st. K1.

2nd row: With White, purl.
3rd row: With Blue, as 1st row.
4th row: With Blue, purl.
Rep last 4 rows 3 times more. 21 sts.
With White, knit 3 rows. Bind off knitwise (**wrong side**).

Sew shoulder seams.
Sew back of Collar to Back neck edge. Sew front of Collar to V-neck edge, leaving Side Edge extensions loose. Insert Side Edge extensions into ring. Sew ring and inset in position to Front. Sew in sleeves. Sew side and sleeve seams. Using damp cloth, steam press pleats into position.

TUNIC

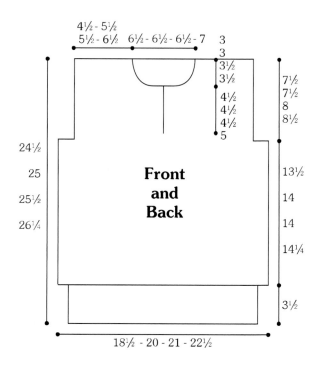

DRESS

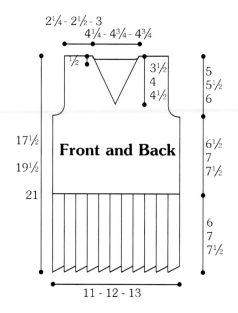

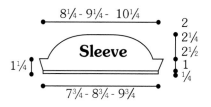

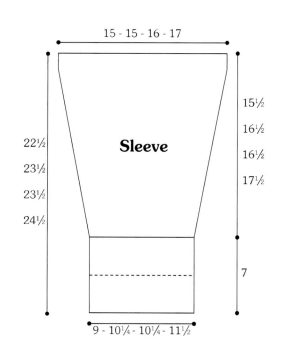

4. Classic Stripes

Easy

SIZES

To fit bust/chest measurement

Small	32-34"
Medium	36-38"
Large	40-42"
Extra-Large	44-46"

Finished bust/chest measurement

Small	37"
Medium	41"
Large	45"
Extra-Large	49"

Size Note: Instructions are written for size Small, with sizes Medium, Large, and Extra-Large in braces { }. Instructions will be easier to read if you circle all the numbers pertaining to your size. If only one number is given, it applies to all sizes.

MATERIALS

Sport Weight Yarn: 1¾ oz (136 yds/50 g)

Sizes	S	M	L	XL	
Ladies' Version					
Blue	5	6	6	7	balls
White	8	9	9	10	balls
Men's Version					
Blue	12	12	13	14	balls
White	2	2	2	2	balls

Samples made with **Patons Grace.**

Size 5 (3.75 mm) knitting needles **or size needed for gauge.** Pair of size 5 (3.75 mm) double-pointed needles for optional drawstring. Size 3 (3.25 mm) knitting needles for neckband of Men's Version only. 2 stitch holders for Men's Version only.

GAUGE SWATCH

24 sts and 32 rows = 4" with larger needles in stocking st.

BACK

With Blue, cast on 111 {123**-135-**147**} sts.
Beg with a knit row, work 13 rows in stocking st.
Next row: (Wrong Side). (Fold line). Knit.**
***Beg with a knit row, cont in stocking st until work from fold line measures 8", ending with right side facing for next row.

Proceed in Stripe Pat as follows:
1st to 4th rows: With White, work 4 rows stocking st.
5th to 8th rows: With Blue, work 4 rows stocking st.
Last 8 rows form Stripe Pat.

Cont in Stripe Pat until work from fold line measures 16½ {**17**-17½-**18**}", ending with right side facing for next row.
Armhole shaping: Keeping cont of Stripe Pat, bind off 9 sts beg next 2 rows. 93 {**105**-117-**129**} sts.

Cont even in Stripe Pat until work from armhole shaping measures approx 1½", ending on an 8th row for Ladies' Version, or on a 4th row for Men's Version.****

Ladies' Version only: With White only, cont even in stocking st, until armhole measures 8½ {**9**-9½-**10**}", ending with **wrong side** facing for next row.

Next row: (Fold line). Knit.
Beg with a knit row, work 6 rows in stocking st. Bind off.***

Men's Version only: With Blue only, cont even in stocking st until armhole measures 8½ {**9**-9½-**10**}", ending with right side facing for next row.

Shoulder shaping: Bind off 12 {**14**-17-**19**} sts beg next 2 rows, then 12 {**15**-17-**20**} sts beg following 2 rows. Leave rem 45 {**47**-49-**51**} sts on a st holder.

FRONT

Men's Version only: Work from ** to **** as given for Back.
With Blue only, cont even in stocking st until armhole measures 5½ {**6**-6¼-**6¾**}", ending with right side facing for next row.

Neck shaping: Next row: K36 {**41**-47-**52**} (neck edge). **Turn.** Leave rem sts on a spare needle.
Dec 1 st at neck edge on next 5 rows, then on following alt rows until there are 24 {**29**-34-**39**} sts.

Cont even until armhole measures same length as Back to beg of shoulder shaping, ending with right side facing for next row.

Shoulder shaping: Bind off 12 {**14**-17-**19**} sts beg next row. Work 1 row even. Bind off rem 12 {**15**-17-**20**} sts.

With right side of work facing, slip next 21 {**23**-23-**25**} sts from spare needle onto a st holder. Join yarn to rem sts and knit to end of row.
Dec 1 st at neck edge on next 5 rows, then on following alt rows until there are 24 {**29**-34-**39**} sts.

Cont even until armhole measures same length as Back to beg of shoulder shaping, ending with **wrong side** facing for next row.

Shoulder shaping: Bind off 12 {**14**-17-**19**} sts beg next row. Work 1 row even. Bind off rem 12 {**15**-17-**20**} sts.

Ladies' Version only: Work from ** to ** as given for Back.
Beg with a knit row, work 4 rows stocking st.

Work eyelets for optional drawstring: Next row: (Right Side). K52 {**58**-64-**70**}. K2tog. yo. K3. yo. Sl1. K1. psso. Knit to end of row.
Next row: Purl.
Work from *** to *** as given for Back.

SLEEVES

Men's Version only: With Blue, cast on 56 {**60**-64-**66**} sts.

Beg with a knit row, work 13 rows in stocking st.
Next row: (Wrong Side). (Fold line). Knit.
Beg with a knit row, cont in stocking st, inc 1 st at each end of needle on 15th row, and every following 4th row, until there are 102 {**108**-114-**120**} sts.
Cont even until work from fold line measures 19 {**20½**-21½-**23**}", ending with right side facing for next row. Bind off.

Ladies' Version only: With White, cast on 60 {**64**-66-**70**} sts.
Beg with a knit row, work 13 rows in stocking st.
Next row: (Wrong Side). (Fold line). Knit.
Beg with a knit row, cont in stocking st and inc 1 st at each end of needle on 15th row, and every following 4th row, until there are 102 {**108**-114-**120**} sts.
Cont even until work from fold line measures 16", ending with right side facing for next row. Bind off.

FINISHING

Pin garment pieces to measurements. Cover with a damp cloth leaving to dry. With **wrong side** facing, sew Front and Back hem facings in position.

Ladies' Version only: With **wrong side** facing, sew neck facings of Front and Back in position.

Shoulder Gussets: (make 2). With White, cast on 15 sts.
Beg with a knit row, work 5 rows stocking st.
Next row: (Wrong Side). (Fold line). Knit.
Beg with a knit row, cont in stocking st, dec 1 st at each end of needle on 7th and every following 4th {**4th**-6th-**6th**} row, until there are 5 {**5**-3-**3**} sts.

Sizes S and M only: Cont in stocking st, dec 1 st at each end of needle on 6th row. 3 sts.

All Sizes: Work 3 rows even. Bind off.

With **wrong side** facing, sew shoulder gussets in position, placing gusset points at armhole edges and sewing side edges of gussets to upper facings on Front and Back, just inside fold lines.

Ladies' and Men's Versions: Place markers 1½" down from bound off edge at each side of sleeve. Sew in sleeves, placing rows above markers between bound off sts at Front and Back armholes to form square armholes. Sew side and sleeve seams. Fold hem along fold line to **wrong side** and sew in position.

Optional Drawstring for Ladies' Version only: With Blue and double-pointed needles, cast on 5 sts. K5. *Slide sts to other end of needle without turning work. K5. Rep from * until work from beg measures 49 {**53**-57-**61**}". Bind off.

Insert drawstring through hem casing at eyelets and knot ends of drawstring.

Men's Version only: Neckband: Sew right shoulder seam. With right side of work facing, smaller needles and Blue, pick up and knit 24 {**24**-25-**25**} sts down Left Front neck edge. K21 {**23**-23-**25**} across Front st holder. Pick up and knit 24 {**24**-25-**25**} sts up Right Front neck edge. K45 {**47**-49-**51**} from Back st holder. 114 {**118**-122-**126**} sts.

1st row: (Wrong Side). *P2. K2. Rep from * to last 2 sts. P2.

2nd row: *K2. P2. Rep from * to last 2 sts. K2.

Rep last 2 rows (K2. P2) ribbing for 1½", ending on a 1st row. Bind off in ribbing. Sew left shoulder and neckband seam.

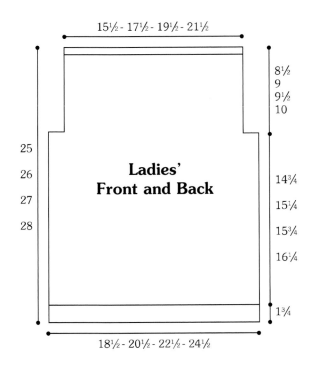

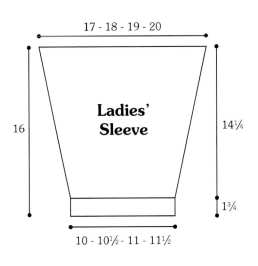

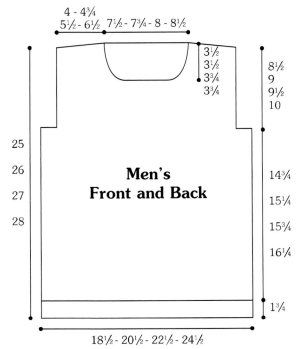

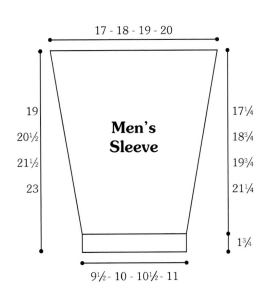

6

5. Guys' Sailing Sweaters

Advanced

SIZES

To fit chest measurement

4	23"
6	25"
8	26½"
Small	30-32"
Medium	34-36"
Large	38-40"
Extra-Large	42-44"

Finished chest measurement

4	30½"
6	32"
8	34½"
Small	42"
Medium	44"
Large	46"
Extra-Large	48"

Size Note: Instructions are written for size Small, with sizes Medium, Large, and Extra-Large in braces { } for the Man's version, and for size 4, with sizes 6 and 8 in braces { } for the Boy's version. Instructions will be easier to read if you circle all the numbers pertaining to your size. If only one number is given, it applies to all sizes.

MATERIALS

Sport Weight Yarn: 1¾ oz (136 yds/50 g)

Sizes	4	6	8	S	M	L	XL	
Beige	12	13	14	25	26	27	28	balls
Red	1	1	1	1	1	1	1	ball
Blue	1	1	1	1	1	1	1	ball

Samples made with **Patons Grace.**

Sizes 7 (4.5 mm) and 8 (5 mm) knitting needles **or size needed for gauge.** Cable needle. 1 stitch holder.

GAUGE SWATCH

22 sts and 26 rows = 4" with 2 strands of yarn and larger needles in cable pat.

STITCH GUIDE

C2B = slip next st onto cable needle and leave at back of work. K1, then K1 from cable needle.
C2F = slip next st onto cable needle and leave at front of work. K1, then K1 from cable needle.
C4B = slip next 2 sts onto cable needle and leave at back of work. K2, then K2 from cable needle.
C4F = slip next 2 sts onto cable needle and leave at front of work. K2, then K2 from cable needle.
T4B = slip next 2 sts onto cable needle and leave at back of work. K2, then P2 from cable needle.
T4F = slip next 2 sts onto cable needle and leave at front of work. P2, then K2 from cable needle.
T3B = slip next st onto cable needle and leave at back of work. K2, then P1 from cable needle.
T3F = slip next 2 sts onto cable needle and leave at front of work. P1, then K2 from cable needle.

PANEL PAT A (worked over 4 sts)
1st row: (Right Side). C2B. C2F.
2nd row: P4.
3rd row: C2F. C2B.
4th row: As 2nd row.
These 4 rows form Panel Pat A.

PANEL PAT B (worked over 10 sts)
1st row: (Right Side). P1. K8. P1.
2nd row: K1. P8. K1.
3rd row: P1. C4B. C4F. P1.
4th row: As 2nd row.
5th and 6th rows: As 1st and 2nd rows.
7th row: P1. T4B. T4F. P1.
8th row: K1. P2. K4. P2. K1.
9th row: T3B. P4. T3F.
10th row: P2. K6. P2.
11th row: K2. P6. K2.
12th row: As 10th row.
13th row: T3F. P4. T3B.
14th row: As 8th row.
15th row: P1. C4F. C4B. P1.
16th row: As 2nd row.
These 16 rows form Panel Pat B.

MAN'S VERSION
BACK
With 2 strands of Red and smaller needles, cast on 92 {96**-102-**106**} sts. Break Red.

With 2 strands of Blue, knit 2 rows, inc 16 {**18**-18-**20**} sts evenly across last row. 108 {**114**-120-**126**} sts. Break Blue.

Next row: (Right Side). With 2 strands of Beige, knit.
Next row: *K3. P3. Rep from * to end of row.
Rep last row 16 times more, inc 7 sts evenly across last row. 115 {**121**-127-**133**} sts.

Change to larger needles and proceed as follows:
Size S only: 1st row: (Right Side). P3. (Work 1st row of Panel Pat A. P3) twice. (Work 1st row of Panel Pat A. P2. Work 1st row of Panel Pat B. P2) twice. Work 1st row of Panel Pat A. P1. (Work 1st row of Panel Pat A. P2. Work 1st row of Panel Pat B. P2) twice. (Work 1st row of Panel Pat A. P3) 3 times.
2nd row: K3. (Work 2nd row of Panel Pat A. K3) twice. (Work 2nd row Panel Pat A. K2. Work 2nd row of Panel Pat B. K2) twice. Work 2nd row of Panel Pat A. K1. (Work 2nd row of Panel Pat A. K2. Work 2nd row of Panel Pat B. K2) twice. (Work 2nd row of Panel Pat A. K3) 3 times.

Sizes M, L and XL only: 1st row: (Right Side). P{**2**-5-**8**}. (Work 1st row of Panel Pat A. P2. Work 1st row of Panel Pat B. P2) 3 times. Work 1st row of Panel Pat A. P1. (Work 1st row of Panel Pat A. P2.

Work 1st row of Panel Pat B. P2) 3 times. Work 1st row of Panel Pat A. P{**2**-5-**8**}.
2nd row: K{**2**-5-**8**}. (Work 2nd row of Panel Pat A. K2. Work 2nd row of Panel Pat B. K2) 3 times. Work 2nd row of Panel Pat A. K1. (Work 2nd row of Panel Pat A. K2. Work 2nd row of Panel Pat B. K2) 3 times. Work 2nd row of Panel Pat A. K{**2**-5-**8**}.

All Sizes: Panel Pat A and Panel Pat B are now in position.**
Cont in pat, keeping cont of Panel Pats, until work from beg measures 26 {**26**-27-**28**}", ending with right side facing for next row.

Shoulder shaping: Bind off 12 {**13**-14-**15**} sts beg next 4 rows, then 13 {**14**-14-**14**} sts beg following 2 rows. Leave rem 41 {**41**-43-**45**} sts on a st holder.

FRONT
Work from ** to ** as given for Back.
Cont in pat, keeping cont of Panel Pats, until work from beg measures 17½ {**17½**-18-**18**}", ending with right side facing for next row.
V-neck shaping: Next row: Pat 57 {**60**-63-**66**} sts. **Turn.** Leave rem sts on a spare needle.
Next row: (**Wrong Side**). Cast on 1 st. Pat to end of row.
Next row: Pat to last 7 sts. Work 2tog. Work appropriate row of Panel Pat A. P1.
Next row: K1. Pat to end of row.
Rep last 2 rows 15 {**15**-16-**14**} times more. 42 {**45**-47-**52**} sts.

Proceed as follows:
Next row: Pat to last 7 sts. Work 2tog. Work appropriate row of Panel Pat A. P1.
Next row: K1. Pat to end of row.
Next row: Pat to last st. P1.
Next row: K1. Pat to end of row.
Rep last 4 rows 4 {**4**-4-**7**} times more. 37 {**40**-42-**44**} sts.

Cont even in pat until Front measures same length as Back to beg of shoulder shaping, ending with right side facing for next row.

Shoulder shaping: Bind off 12 {**13**-14-**15**} sts beg next and following alt row. Work 1 row even. Bind off rem 13 {**14**-14-**14**} sts.

With right side of work facing, slip next st onto a safety pin. Join 2 strands of Beige to rem sts.
Next row: Cast on 1 st. Pat to end of row. Work 1 row even.

Proceed as follows:
Next row: (Right Side). P1. Work Panel Pat A. Work 2tog. Pat to end of row.
Next row: Pat to last st. K1.
Rep last 2 rows 15 {**15**-16-**14**} times more. 42 {**45**-47-**52**} sts.

Next row: (Right Side). P1. Work Panel Pat A. Work 2tog. Pat to end of row.
Next row: Pat to last st. K1.
Next row: P1. Pat to end of row.
Next row: Pat to last st. K1.
Rep last 4 rows 4 {**4**-4-**7**} times more. 37 {**40**-42-**44**} sts.

Cont even in pat until Front measures same length as Back to beg of shoulder shaping, ending with **wrong side** facing for next row.

Shoulder shaping: Bind off 12 {**13**-14-**15**} sts beg next and following alt row. Work 1 row even. Bind off rem 13 {**14**-14-**14**} sts.

SLEEVES
With smaller needles and 2 strands of Red, cast on 55 sts. Break Red.
With 2 strands of Blue, knit 2 rows, inc 8 sts evenly across last row. 63 sts. Break Blue.
1st row: (Right Side). With 2 strands of Beige, knit.
2nd row: P3. *K3. P3. Rep from * to end of row.
3rd row: K3. *P3. K3. Rep from * to end of row.
Rep last 2 rows 7 times more, then 2nd row once, inc 7 sts evenly across last row. 70 sts.
Change to larger needles and proceed in pattern as follows:
1st row: (Right Side). P1. (Work 1st row of Panel Pat A. P3) twice. (Work 1st row of Panel Pat A. P2. Work 1st row of Panel Pat B. P2) twice. (Work 1st row of Panel Pat A. P3) twice. Work 1st row of Panel Pat A. P1.
2nd row: K1. (Work 2nd row of Panel Pat A. K3) twice. (Work 2nd row of Panel Pat A. K2. Work 2nd row of Panel Pat B. K2) twice. (Work 2nd row of Panel Pat A. K3) twice. Work 2nd row of Panel Pat A. K1.
Panel Pat A and Panel Pat B are now in position.

Cont in pat, keeping cont of Panel Pats, inc 1 st at each end of next and following 6th {**6th**-4th-**4th**} rows to 94 {**98**-80-**98**} sts, taking inc sts into reps of Panel Pat A bordered by 3 sts of reverse stocking st.

Sizes L and XL only: Inc 1 st at each end of every following 6th row to {104-**110**} sts, taking inc sts into reps of Panel Pat A bordered by 3 sts of reverse stocking st.

All Sizes: Cont even until Sleeve from beg measures 18 {**18**-19-**19**}", ending with right side facing for next row. Bind off.

FINISHING
Pin garment pieces to measurements and cover with a damp cloth allowing cloth to dry.

Neckband: Sew right shoulder seam. With right side of work facing, smaller needles and 2 strands of Beige, pick up and knit 52 {**52**-58-**64**} sts down Left Front of V-neck. P1 from safety pin (mark this st). Pick up and knit 51 {**51**-57-**63**} sts up Right Front of V-neck. K41 {**41**-43-**45**} from Back st holder, dec 4 {**4**-6-**2**} sts evenly across. 141 {**141**-153-**171**} sts.

1st row: (Wrong Side). *P3. K3. Rep from * to 4 sts before marked st. P2. P2tog. K1. P2togtbl. P2. *K3. P3. Rep from * to last 3 sts. K3.
2nd row: Work in (K3. P3) ribbing to 2 sts before marked st. Work 2tog. K1. Work 2tog. Work in (K3. P3) ribbing to end of row.
Rep last row 3 times more.

Change to 2 strands of Blue and knit 2 rows, dec 1 st each side of marked st, as before, on both rows.

Change to 2 strands of Red and knit 1 row, dec 1 st each side of marked st, as before. Bind off.

Sew left shoulder and neckband seam.
Place markers 8½ {**9**-9½-**10**}" down from shoulder seams on sides of Back and Front. Sew in sleeves between markers. Sew side and sleeve seams.

BOY'S VERSION
BACK
***With smaller needles and 2 strands of Red, cast on 66 {**70**-76} sts. Break Red.
With 2 strands of Blue, knit 2 rows, inc 12 {**12**-14} sts evenly across last row. 78 {**82**-90} sts. Break Blue.

Next row: (Right Side). With 2 strands of Beige, knit.
Next row: *K2. P2. Rep from * to last 2 sts. K2.
Next row: *P2. K2. Rep from * to last 2 sts. P2.
Rep last 2 rows 5 times more, then 2nd row once, inc 7 {**7**-5} sts evenly across last row. 85 {**89**-95} sts.

Change to larger needles and proceed in pat as follows:
1st row: (Right Side). P2 {**4**-7}. (Work 1st row of Panel Pat A. P2. Work 1st row of Panel Pat B. P2) twice. Work 1st row of Panel Pat A. P1. (Work 1st row of Panel Pat A. P2. Work 1st row of Panel Pat B. P2) twice. Work 1st row of Panel Pat A. P2 {**4**-7}.
2nd row: K2 {**4**-7}. (Work 2nd row of Panel Pat A. K2. Work 2nd row of Panel Pat B. K2) twice. Work 2nd row of Panel Pat A. K1. (Work 2nd row of Panel Pat A. K2. Work 2nd row of Panel Pat B. K2) twice. Work 2nd row of Panel Pat A. K2 {**4**-7}.
Panel Pat A and Panel Pat B are now in position.***

Cont in pat, keeping cont of Panel Pats, until work from beg measures 17 {**19**-20½}", ending with right side facing for next row.

Shoulder shaping: Bind off 10 {**11**-12} sts beg next 4 rows. Bind off 11 sts beg following 2 rows. Leave rem 23 {**23**-25} sts on a st holder.

FRONT
Work from *** to *** as given for Back.
Cont in pat, keeping cont of Panel Pats, until work from beg measures 11 {**12½**-13½}", ending with right side facing for next row.

V-neck shaping: Next row: Pat across 42 {**44**-47} sts. **Turn.** Leave rem sts on a spare needle.
Next row: Cast on 1 st. Pat to end of row.
Next row: Pat to last 7 sts. P2tog. Work appropriate row of Panel Pat A. P1.
Next row: K1. Pat to end of row.
Rep last 2 rows 5 {**4**-4} times more. 37 {**40**-43} sts.

Proceed as follows:
Next row: Pat to last 7 sts. P2tog. Work appropriate row of Panel Pat A. P1.
Next row: K1. Pat to end of row.
Next row: Pat to last 5 sts. Work appropriate row of Panel Pat A. P1.
Next row: K1. Pat to end of row.
Rep last 4 rows 5 {**6**-7} times more. 31 {**33**-35} sts.

Cont even in pat until Front measures same length as Back to beg of shoulder shaping, ending with right side facing for next row.

Shoulder shaping: Bind off 10 {**11**-12} sts beg next and following alt row. Work 1 row even. Bind off rem 11 sts.
With right side of work facing, slip next st onto a safety pin. Join 2 strands of Beige to rem sts.
Next row: Cast on 1 st. Pat to end of row.
Work 1 row even.

Proceed as follows:
Next row: (Right Side). P1. Work appropriate row of Panel Pat A. P2togtbl. Pat to end of row.
Next row: Pat to last st. K1.
Rep last 2 rows 5 {**4**-4} times more. 37 {**40**-43} sts.

Proceed as follows:
Next row: (Right Side). P1. Work appropriate row of Panel Pat A. P2togtbl. Pat to end of row.
Next row: Pat to last st. K1.
Next row: P1. Pat to end of row.
Next row: Pat to last st. K1.
Rep last 4 rows 5 {**6**-7} times more. 31 {**33**-35} sts.

Cont even in pat until Front measures same length as Back to beg of shoulder shaping, ending with **wrong side** facing for next row.

Shoulder shaping: Bind off 10 {**11**-12} sts beg next and following alt row. Work 1 row even. Bind off rem 11 sts.

SLEEVES
With smaller needles and 2 strands of Red, cast on 32 sts. Break Red.
With 2 strands of Blue, knit 2 rows, inc 6 sts evenly across last row. 38 sts. Break Blue.
1st row: (Right Side). With 2 strands of Beige, knit.
2nd row: *K2. P2. Rep from * to last 2 sts. K2.
3rd row: *P2. K2. Rep from * to last 2 sts. P2.
Rep last 2 rows 5 times more, then 2nd row once, inc 4 sts evenly across last row. 42 sts.
Change to larger needles and proceed in pat as follows:
1st row: (Right Side). P1. (Work 1st row of Panel Pat A. P2. Work 1st row of Panel Pat B. P2) twice. Work 1st row of Panel Pat A. P1.

2nd row: K1. (Work 2nd row of Panel Pat A. K2. Work 2nd row of Panel Pat B. K2) twice. Work 2nd row of Panel Pat A. K1.

Panel Pat A and Panel Pat B are now in position.

Cont in pat, keeping cont of Panel Pats, inc 1 st at each end of next and every following alt row to 48 {**54**-60} sts, then every following 4th row to 68 {**72**-78} sts, taking inc sts into reps of Panel Pat A, bordered by 3 sts of reverse stocking st.

Cont even until Sleeve from beg measures 10$\frac{1}{2}$ {**12**-13$\frac{1}{2}$}", ending with right side facing for next row. Bind off.

FINISHING

Pin garment pieces to measurements and cover with a damp cloth allowing cloth to dry.

Neckband: Sew right shoulder seam. With right side of work facing, smaller needles and 2 strands of Beige, pick up and knit 37 {**41**-45} sts down Left Front of V-neck. P1 from safety pin (mark this st). Pick up and knit 37 {**41**-45} sts up Right Front of V-neck. K23 {**23**-25} from Back st holder, dec 1 (**dec 1**-inc 1) st at center. 97 {**105**-117} sts.

1st row: (**Wrong Side**). *P2. K2. Rep from * to 3 sts before marked st. P1. P2tog. K1. P2togtbl. P1. K2. *P2. K2. Rep from * to end of row.

2nd and 3rd rows: Work in (K2. P2) ribbing to 2 sts before marked st. Work 2tog. K1. Work 2tog. Work in (K2. P2) ribbing to end of row.

Change to 2 strands of Blue and knit 2 rows, dec 1 st each side of marked st, as before, on both rows.

Change to 2 strands of Red and knit 1 row, dec 1 st each side of marked st, as before. Bind off.

Sew left shoulder and neckband seam.
Place markers 6 {**6$\frac{1}{2}$**-7}" down from shoulder seams on sides of Back and Front. Sew in sleeves between markers. Sew side and sleeve seams.

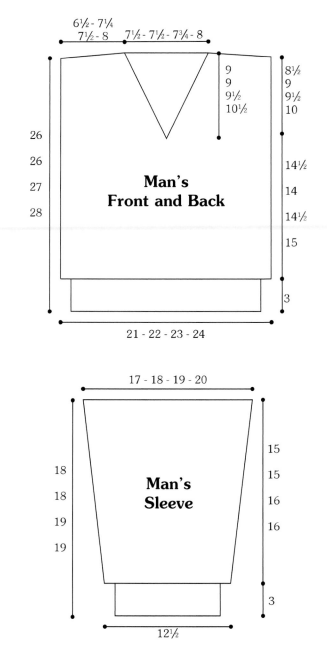

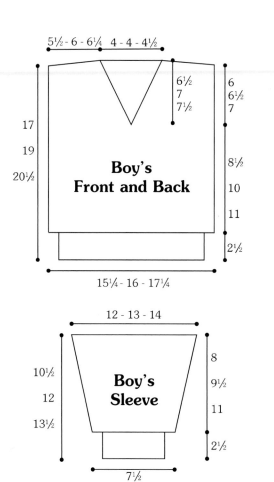

6. Mom & Me Skater Wear

Easy

SIZES

LADY'S SKATER CARDIGAN
Bust/chest measurement

Small	30-32"
Medium	34-36"
Large	38-40"
Extra-Large	42-44"

Finished bust/chest

Small	40"
Medium	44"
Large	48"
Extra-Large	51"

GIRL'S SKATER OUTFIT
JACKET
Chest measurement

4	23"
6	25"
8	26½"
10	28"

Finished chest

4	28"
6	31"
8	32"
10	35"

SKIRT
Waist measurement

4	21"
6	22"
8	23"
10	24"

Finished waist

4	21"
6	22½"
8	24"
10	25½"

HAT and MITTS
To fit child ages: 4-6 (**8-10**) yrs.

Size Note: *The instructions for the Lady's Cardigan are written for Small, with sizes Medium, Large and Extra-Large in braces { }. The instructions for the Girl's Skater Outfit are written for size 4, with sizes 6, 8 and 10 in braces { }. Instructions will be easier to read if you circle all the numbers pertaining to your size. If only one number is given, it applies to all sizes.*

MATERIALS

CARDIGAN
Worsted Weight Yarn: 3½ oz (223 yds/100g)

Sizes	S	M	L	XL	
White	7	7	8	8	balls
Dark Purple	1	1	1	1	ball
Green	1	1	1	1	ball
Pink	1	1	1	1	ball
Grey	1	1	1	1	ball
Blue	1	1	1	1	ball
Soft Purple	1	1	1	1	ball

Sample is made with **Patons Classic Merino Wool.**

Sizes 5 (3.75 mm) and 7 (4.5 mm) knitting needles **or size needed for gauge.** Separating zipper. Tapestry needle for duplicate stitching.

GIRL'S SKATER OUTFIT
Worsted Weight Yarn: 3½ oz (210 yds/100g)

GIRL'S JACKET

Sizes	4	6	8	10	
Blue	3	4	4	5	balls
White	1	1	1	1	ball

SKIRT

Sizes	4	6	8	10	
Blue	2	2	3	3	balls
White	1	1	1	1	ball

HAT and MITTS

Sizes	4/6	8/10	
Blue	1	1	ball
White	1	1	ball

Samples are made with **Patons Décor**.

Sizes 5 (3.75 mm) and 7 (4.5 mm) knitting needles, sizes 5 (3.75 mm) and 7 (4.5 mm) circular knitting needles 24" long **or size needed for gauge.** Separating zipper for Jacket. 1 st holder. 1 yd of elastic 1¼" wide for Skirt.

GAUGE SWATCH

20 sts and 26 rows = 4" with larger needles in stocking st.

STITCH GUIDE

> **ML** = Make loop. Knit into the next st **do not** drop st from needle. yf, wind yarn around left thumb, yb, knit into same st (2 sts made). Slip 2 sts just made onto right-hand needle.
> **yf** = Yarn forward.
> **yb** = Yarn back.
> **K1B** = Knit into back of next st.
> **M1** = Make one st by picking up horizontal loop lying before next st and knitting into back of loop.

CARDIGAN
BACK
With smaller needles and White, cast on 91 {**101**-111-**119**} sts.
1st row: K1. *P1. K1. Rep from * to end of row.
2nd row: P1. *K1. P1. Rep from * to end of row.
Rep last 2 rows (K1. P1) ribbing for 3", ending on a 2nd row and inc 10 sts evenly across last row. 101 {**111**-121-**129**} sts.

Change to larger needles and proceed in stocking st until work from beg measures 25½ {**26**-26½-**27**}", ending with right side facing for next row.

Shoulder shaping: Bind off 11 {**13**-14-**15**} sts beg next 4 rows, then 12 {**12**-14-**16**} sts beg following 2 rows. Bind off rem 33 {**35**-37-**37**} sts.

LEFT FRONT
With smaller needles and White, cast on 45 {51**-55-**59**} sts.
Work 3" in (K1. P1) ribbing, as given for Back, ending on a 2nd row and inc 5 {**4**-5-**5**} sts evenly across last row. 50 {**55**-60-**64**} sts.**

Change to larger needles and proceed as follows:
1st row: (Right Side). Knit.
2nd row: K2. Purl to end of row.
Rep last 2 rows until work from beg measures 22¼ {**22¾**-23-**23½**}", ending with **wrong side** facing for next row.

Neck shaping: Bind off 8 {**8**-9-**9**} sts beg next row. Purl to end of row.
Dec 1 st at neck edge on next 3 rows, then on following alt rows to 34 {**38**-42-**46**} sts.

Cont even in stocking st until work from beg measures same length as Back to beg of shoulder shaping, ending with right side facing for next row.

Shoulder shaping: Bind off 11 {**13**-14-**15**} sts beg next and following alt row. Work 1 row even. Bind off rem 12 {**12**-14-**16**} sts.

RIGHT FRONT
Work from ** to ** as given for Left Front.

Change to larger needles and proceed as follows:
1st row: (Right Side). Knit.
2nd row: Purl to last 2 sts. K2.
Rep last 2 rows until work from beg measures 22¼ {**22¾**-23-**23½**}", ending with right side facing for next row.

Neck shaping: Bind off 8 {**8**-9-**9**} sts beg next row. Knit to end of row.
Work 1 row even.
Dec 1 st at neck edge on next 3 rows, then on following alt rows to 34 {**38**-42-**46**} sts.

Cont even in stocking st until work from beg measures same length as Back to beg of shoulder shaping, ending with **wrong side** facing for next row.

Shoulder shaping: Bind off 11 {**13**-14-**15**} sts beg next and following alt row. Work 1 row even. Bind off rem 12 {**12**-14-**16**} sts.

SLEEVES
With smaller needles and White, cast on 39 {**39**-41-**41**} sts.
Work 3" in (K1. P1) ribbing as given for Back, ending on a 2nd row and inc 18 sts evenly across last row. 57 {**57**-59-**59**} sts.

Change to larger needles and proceed in stocking st, inc 1 st each end of needle on 5th and every following 4th {**2nd**-4th-**2nd**} row to 95 {**67**-101-**69**} sts.

Sizes M and XL only: Inc 1 st each end of needle on every following 4th row to {**101**-105} sts.

All Sizes: Cont even until work from beg measures 17½ {**18**-18½-**19**}", ending with right side facing for next row. Bind off.

COLLAR
With smaller needles and White, cast on 4 {**4**-6-**6**} sts.
1st row: K1. M1. Knit to last st. M1. K1.
2nd row: Knit.
Rep last 2 rows 11 times more. 28 {**28**-30-**30**} sts.
Next row: (Outside edge). K1. M1. Knit to end of row.
Knit 5 rows even.
Rep last 6 rows 3 times more. 32 {**32**-34-**34**} sts.

Cont even in garter st until work from beginning measures 14¾ {**15¼**-15¾-**15¾**}", ending at outside edge.
Next row: K1. K2tog. Knit to end of row.
Knit 5 rows even.
Rep last 6 rows 3 times more.

Next row: K1. K2tog. Knit to last 3 sts. K2tog. K1.
Next row: Knit.
Rep last 2 rows to 4 {**4**-6-**6**} sts. Bind off.

FINISHING
Pin all garment pieces to measurements. Cover with a damp cloth leaving to dry.

Following Chart I, embroider skater on Right Front using duplicate st. *Chart I is shown on page 37. (See Duplicate Stitch Diagram on page 36).*

Sew shoulder seams. Place markers on side edges of Front and Back 9½ {**10**-10-**10½**}" down from shoulder seams. Sew in sleeves between markers. Sew side and sleeve seams. Sew neck edge of collar to neck edge of cardigan placing cast on and bound off ends along bound off sts at neck edge of cardigan. Sew zipper in position. **Do not press.**

GIRL'S JACKET
BACK
With larger needles and Blue, cast on 71 {**77**-81-**87**} sts.
Work 1" in stocking st, ending with **wrong side facing for next row.
Next row: (Fold row). Knit. **
Beg with a knit row, work in stocking st until work from fold row measures 14 {**15½**-17-**18½**}", ending with right side facing for next row.

Shape shoulders: Bind off 8 {**8**-9-**9**} sts beg next 4 rows, then 7 {**9**-8-**9**} sts beg following 2 rows. Leave rem 25 {**27**-29-**33**} sts on a st holder.

LEFT FRONT
With larger needles and Blue, cast on 35 {**37**-39-**43**} sts. Work from ** to ** as given for Back.

Proceed as follows:
1st row: (Right Side). Knit.
2nd row: K2. Purl to end of row.

Rep last 2 rows until work from fold row measures 12 {**13**-14½-**16**}", ending with **wrong side** facing for next row.

Shape neck: Bind off 7 {**7**-8-**9**} sts beg next row. Dec 1 st at neck edge on next and following alt rows to 23 {**25**-26-**27**} sts.

Cont even until work from fold row measures same length as Back to beg of shoulder shaping, ending with right side facing for next row.

Shoulder shaping: Bind off 8 {**8**-9-**9**} sts beg next and following alt row. Work 1 row even. Bind off rem 7 {**9**-8-**9**} sts.

RIGHT FRONT

With larger needles and Blue, cast on 35 {**37**-39-**43**} sts. Work from ** to ** as given for Back.

Proceed as follows:
1st row: (Right Side). Knit.
2nd row: Purl to last 2 sts. K2.

Rep last 2 rows until work from fold row measures 12 {**13**-14½-**16**}", ending with right side facing for next row.

Shape neck: Bind off 7 {**7**-8-**9**} sts beg next row. Work 1 row even.
Dec 1 st at neck edge on next and following alt rows to 23 {**25**-26-**27**} sts.

Cont even until work from fold row measures same length as Back to beg of shoulder shaping, ending with **wrong side** facing for next row.

Shoulder shaping: Bind off 8 {**8**-9-**9**} sts beg next and following alt row. Work 1 row even. Cast off rem 7 {**9**-8-**9**} sts.

SLEEVES

With larger needles and Blue, cast on 43 {**43**-45-**45**} sts. Work from ** to ** as given for Back.

Work in stocking st, inc 1 st each end of needle on 3rd and every following 4th row to 71 {**75**-81-**85**} sts.

Cont even until work from fold row measures 11 {**13**-14½-**16**}", ending with right side facing for next row. Bind off.

COLLAR

Sew shoulder seams. With right side of work facing, White and smaller needles, pick up and knit 20 {**22**-22-**25**} sts up Right Front neck edge, knit across 25 {**27**-29-**33**} sts from Back st holder, dec 2 sts evenly across. Pick up and knit 20 {**22**-22-**25**} sts down Left Front neck edge. 63 {**69**-71-**81**} sts.

Proceed as follows:
1st row: (Wrong Side). K1. *ML. K1. Rep from * to end of row.
2nd row: P1. *P2tog. P1. Rep from * to end of row.
3rd row: K2. *ML. K1. Rep from * to last st. K1.
4th row: P2. *P2tog. P1. Rep from * to last st. P1.

Rep last 4 rows for 3", ending with **wrong side** facing for next row. Bind off.

FINISHING

Place markers on side edges of Front and Back 7 {**7½**-8-**8½**}" down from shoulder seams. Sew in sleeves between markers. Sew side and sleeve seams. Sew zipper in position. Fold bottom of Back, Fronts and Sleeves along fold row to **wrong side**. Sew cast on edge in position.

SKIRT

Note: Skirt is worked from bottom to top.

With White and larger circular needle, cast on 213 {**229**-245-**261**} sts. Join in rnd, taking care not to twist and proceed as follows:
***1st rnd:** (Right Side). K1. *ML. K1. Rep from * around.
2nd rnd: K1. *K2tog. K1. Rep from * around.
3rd rnd: K2. *ML. K1. Rep from * to last st. ML.
4th rnd: K2. *K2tog. K1. Rep from * to last 2 sts. K2tog.**
Rep from ** to ** twice more.
Dec 1 st at center of last rnd. 212 {**228**-244-**260**} sts.

Change to Blue and proceed in stocking st until work from beg measures 10 {**11½**-12½-**13½**}".

Shape waist: *K1. K3tog. Rep from * around. 106 {**114**-122-**130**} sts.
Change to smaller circular needle and work 3" in stocking st. Bind off.

FINISHING

Fold waistband in half and sew in position leaving an opening for elastic. Cut elastic to waist measurement and thread through opening. Secure ends of elastic and sew opening closed.

HAT

With White and larger needles, cast on 93 {**105**} sts.
***1st row:** (Right Side). K1. *ML. K1. Rep from * to end of row.
2nd row: P1. *P2tog. P1. Rep from * to end of row.
3rd row: K2. *ML. K1. Rep from * to last st. K1.
4th row: P2. *P2tog. P1. Rep from * to last st. P1.**
Rep from ** to ** twice more, dec 4 {**5**} sts evenly across last row. 89 {**100**} sts.

Change to Blue and proceed as follows:
1st row: K1. *K2tog. K9. Rep from * to end of row. 81 {**91**} sts.
2nd row: Purl.
3rd row: K1. *K2tog. K8. Rep from * to end of row. 73 {**82**} sts.
4th row: Purl.
Cont in this manner, dec 8 {**9**} sts evenly across next and following alt rows until 17 {**19**} sts rem. Break yarn leaving a long end. Draw end through rem sts and fasten securely.

MITTS
RIGHT MITT
Cuff: With White and larger needles, cast on 33 {**37**} sts. Work from ** to ** twice as given for Hat, dec 1 st at center of last row.
Change to Blue and work 6 rows in stocking st.
Shape thumb: 1st row: K17 {**19**}. Inc 1 st in each of next 2 sts. Knit to end of row.
2nd and alt rows: Purl.
3rd row: K17 {**19**}. Inc 1 st in next st. K2. Inc 1 st in next st. Knit to end of row.
5th row: K17 {**19**}. Inc 1 st in next st. K4. Inc 1 st in next st. Knit to end of row.

Cont in this manner, having 2 sts more between inc for thumb gusset every alt row to 40 {**46**} sts. Purl 1 row.

Make thumb: K27 {**31**}. **Turn.** Cast on 1 st. P10 {**12**} including cast on st. **Turn.** **Cast on 1 st. Working on these 11 {**13**} sts cont even for 1½ {**1¾**}", ending with a right side facing for next row.

Next row: K1. *K2tog. Rep from * to end of row. Break yarn. Thread end through rem sts. Draw up and fasten securely. Sew thumb seam.

With right side of work facing, join yarn to last st on right-hand needle. Pick up and knit 2 sts at base of thumb. Knit across sts on left-hand needle.
Next row: Purl across, purling tog the 2 sts picked up at base of thumb. 32 {**36**} sts.
Cont even until work from beg measures 4¼ {**5¼**}", ending with right side facing for next row.

Shape top: 1st row: K1. Sl1K. K1. psso. K10 {**12**}. K2tog. K2. Sl1K. K1. psso. Knit to last 3 sts. K2tog. K1.
2nd and alt rows: Purl.

3rd row: K1. Sl1K. K1. psso. K8 {**10**}. K2tog. K2. Sl1K. K1. psso. Knit to last 3 sts. K2tog. K1.
5th row: K1. Sl1K. K1. psso. K6 {**8**}. K2tog. K2. Sl1K. K1. psso. Knit to last 3 sts. K2tog. K1.
Cont in this manner, having 2 sts fewer between decs every alt row to 16 sts. Bind off purlwise. Sew top and side seam.

LEFT MITT
With White, work Cuff as given for Right Mitt.

Change to Blue and work 6 rows in stocking st.
Shape thumb: 1st row: K12 {**14**}. Inc 1 st in each of next 2 sts. Knit to end of row.
2nd and alt rows: Purl.
3rd row: K12 {**14**}. Inc 1 st in next st. K2. Inc 1 st in next st. Knit to end of row.
5th row: K12 {**14**}. Inc 1 st in next st. K4. Inc 1 st in next st. Knit to end of row.

Cont in this manner, having 2 sts more between incs for thumb gusset every alt row to 40 {**46**} sts. Purl 1 row.

Make thumb: K22 {**26**}. **Turn.** Cast on 1 st. P10 {**12**} including cast on st. **Turn.** Cast on 1 st. Working on these 11 (**13**) sts, finish thumb and remainder of Mitt as given for Right Mitt.

DUPLICATE STITCH

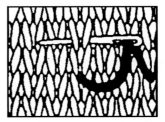

Bring needle up through centre of stitch from back of work and * insert from right to left behind stitch immediately above.

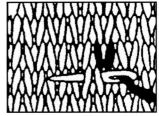

Bring needle down through center of original stitch and out through center of next stitch to be worked.

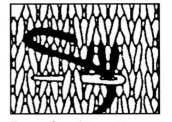

Repeat from * to continue.

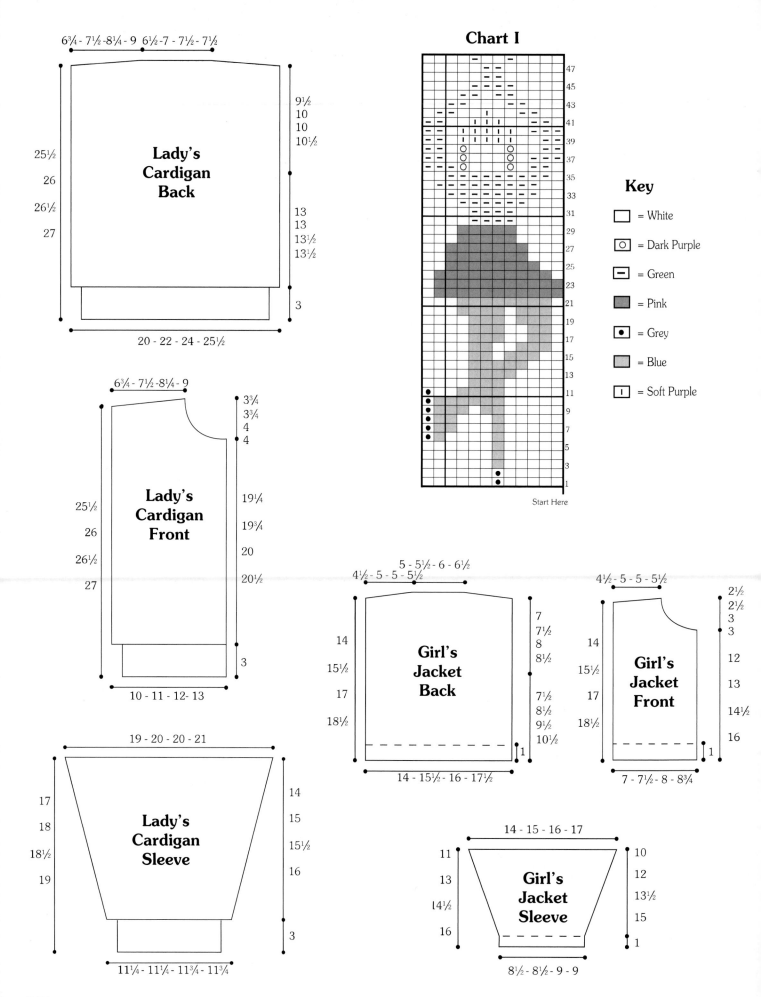

Chart I

Key

☐ = White

⊙ = Dark Purple

⊟ = Green

▨ = Pink

⊡ = Grey

▢ = Blue

Ⅰ = Soft Purple

Start Here

Lady's Cardigan Back

6¾ - 7½ -8¼ - 9 6½ -7 - 7½ - 7½

9½
10
10
10½

25½
26
26½
27

13
13
13½
13½

3

20 - 22 - 24 - 25½

Lady's Cardigan Front

6¾ - 7½ -8¼ - 9

3¾
3¾
4
4

25½
26
26½
27

19¼

19¾

20

20½

3

10 - 11 - 12- 13

Lady's Cardigan Sleeve

19 - 20 - 20 - 21

17
18
18½
19

14

15

15½

16

3

11¼ - 11¼ - 11¾ - 11¾

Girl's Jacket Back

5 - 5½ - 6 - 6½
4½ - 5 - 5 - 5½

7
7½
8
8½

14

15½

17

18½

7½
8½
9½
10½

1

14 - 15½ - 16 - 17½

Girl's Jacket Front

4½ - 5 - 5 - 5½

2½
2½
3
3

14

15½

17

18½

12

13

14½

16

1

7 - 7½ - 8 - 8¾

Girl's Jacket Sleeve

14 - 15 - 16 - 17

11

13

14½

16

10

12

13½

15

1

8½ - 8½ - 9 - 9

37

8

9

10

41

7. Lady's & Girl's Cable Cardigans   Intermediate

SIZES

LADY'S
Bust/Chest measurement

Small	30-32"
Medium	34-36"
Large/Extra-Large	38-44"

Finished bust/chest

Small	38"
Medium	41"
Large/Extra-Large	50"

GIRL'S
Chest measurement

4	23"
6	25"
8	26½"

Finished chest

4	27"
6	33"
8	35"

Size Note: *The instructions for the Lady's Cardigan are written for Small, with sizes Medium and Large/Extra-Large in braces { }. The instructions for the Girl's Cardigan are written for size 4, with sizes 6 and 8 in braces { }. Instructions will be easier to read if you circle all the numbers pertaining to your size. If only one number is given, it applies to all sizes.*

MATERIALS

Worsted Weight Yarn: 3½ oz (223 yds/100g)

LADY'S

Sizes	S	M	L/XL	
Grey	10	11	11	balls

GIRL'S

Sizes	4	6	8	
Rich Red	4	4	5	balls

Samples made with **Patons Classic Merino Wool.**

Sizes 5 (3.75 mm) and 7 (4.5 mm) knitting needles **or size needed for gauge**. Five buttons for Lady's Cardigan. Five buttons for Girl's Cardigan. 1 st holder. Cable needle.

GAUGE SWATCH
20 sts and 26 rows = 4" in stocking st.

STITCH GUIDE

> **C6B** = slip next 3 sts onto a cable needle and leave at back of work. K3, then K3 from cable needle.
> **C6F** = slip next 3 sts onto a cable needle and leave at front of work. K3, then K3 from cable needle.
> **C4B** = slip next 2 sts onto a cable needle and leave at back of work. K2, then K2 from cable needle.
> **C4F** = slip next 2 sts onto a cable needle and leave at front of work. K2, then K2 from cable needle.

LADY'S CARDIGAN
BACK
With smaller needles, cast on 98 {**128**-158} sts. Work 9 rows garter st (knit every row), noting that first row is **wrong side**, and inc 25 sts evenly across last row. 123 {**153**-183} sts.

Change to larger needles and proceed in pat as follows:
1st row: (Right Side). Knit.
2nd row: K3. *P12. K3. Rep from * to end of row.
3rd and 4th rows: As 1st and 2nd rows once more.
5th row: K3. *C6B. C6F. K3. Rep from * to end of row.
6th row: As 2nd row.
7th and 8th rows: As 1st and 2nd rows once more.
These 8 rows form pat.

Cont in pat until work from beg measures 17½ {**18**-18½}", ending with right side facing for next row.

Armhole shaping: Keeping cont of pat, bind off 9 sts beg of next 2 rows. 105 {**135**-165} sts.

Cont in pat until work from beg measures 26½ {**27**½-28½}", ending with right side facing for next row.

Next row: Bind off 29 {**39**-51} sts at beg of next 2 rows. Leave rem 47 {**57**-63} sts on a st holder.

LEFT FRONT
With smaller needles, cast on 68 {**68**-80} sts. Work 9 rows garter st, noting that 1st row is **wrong side**, and inc 12 {**12**-15} sts evenly across last row. 80 {**80**-95} sts.

Change to larger needles and proceed in pat as follows:
1st row: (Right Side). Knit.
2nd row: K5. *P12. K3. Rep from * to end of row.
3rd and 4th rows: As 1st and 2nd rows once more.
5th row: *K3. C6B. C6F. Rep from * to last 5 sts. K5.
6th row: As 2nd row.
7th and 8th rows: As 1st and 2nd rows once more.
These 8 rows form pat.

Cont in pat until work from beg measures 17½ {**18**-18½}", ending with right side facing for next row.

Armhole shaping: Keeping cont of pat, bind off 9 sts beg next row. 71 {**71**-86} sts.

Cont in pat until work from beg measures 24 {**25**-26}", ending with **wrong side** facing for next row.

Neck shaping: Next row: Bind off 18 sts (neck edge). Pat to end of row.
Keeping cont of pat, dec 1 st at neck edge on next 11 rows, then every alt row until there are 29 {**39**-51} sts.

Cont even until work from beg measures same length as Back to shoulder, ending with right side facing for next row. Bind off.

Place markers for five buttons along button band on Left Front, having top button ½" down from neck shaping and bottom button ½" above cast-on edge and rem 3 buttons spaced evenly between.

RIGHT FRONT
With smaller needles, cast on 68 {**68**-80} sts. Work 5 rows garter st, noting that first row is **wrong side.**
Next row: (Right Side). (Buttonhole row). K2. Bind off 2 sts. Knit to end of row.
Next row: Knit, casting on 2 sts over bound off sts. Work a further 2 rows garter st, inc 12 {**12**-15} sts evenly across last row. 80 {**80**-95} sts.

Note: Buttonholes are worked on Right Front to correspond to button markers on Left Front as follows:
Next row: (Right Side). K2. Bind off 2 sts. K1. Pat to end of row.
Next row: Work in pat, casting on 2 sts over bound off sts.

Change to larger needles and proceed in pat as follows:
1st row: (Right Side). Knit.
2nd row: *K3. P12. Rep from * to last 5 sts. K5.
3rd and 4th rows: As 1st and 2nd rows once more.
5th row: K5. *C6B. C6F. K3. Rep from * to end of row.
6th row: As 2nd row.
7th and 8th rows: As 1st and 2nd rows once more.
These 8 rows form pat.

Cont in pat until work from beg measures 17½ {**18**-18½}", ending with **wrong side** facing for next row.

Armhole shaping: Keeping cont of pat, bind off 9 sts beg next row. 56 {**56**-71} sts.

Cont in pat until work from beg measures 24 {**25**-26}", ending with right side facing for next row.

Neck shaping: Next row: Bind off 18 sts (neck edge). Pat to end of row.
Keeping cont of pat, dec 1 st at neck edge on next 11 rows, then every alt row until there are 29 {**39**-51} sts.

Cont even until work from beg measures same length as Back to shoulder, ending with **wrong side** facing for next row. Bind off.

SLEEVES

With smaller needles, cast on 51 sts. Work 9 rows garter st, noting that first row is **wrong side**, and inc 27 sts evenly across last row. 78 sts.

Change to larger needles and proceed in pat as given for Back, inc 1 st at each end of needle on next and every following 4th row to 100 {**126**-128} sts, then every 6th row to 134 {**142**-150} sts, taking inc sts into pat until you have 8 complete cable reps, then taking inc sts into garter st.

Cont even until work from beg measures 21½", ending with right side facing for next row.
Bind off.

FINISHING

Pin garment pieces to measurements and cover with a damp cloth, leaving to dry.

Collar: Sew shoulder seams. With right side of work facing and smaller needles, beginning at center of button band, pick up and knit 30 {**32**-34} sts up Right Front neck edge. Knit across 47 {**57**-63} sts from Back st holder, dec 7 sts evenly across. Pick up and knit 30 {**32**-34} sts down Left Front neck edge, ending at center of button band. 100 {**114**-124} sts. Work garter st until collar from beg measures 3". Bind off.

Place markers 1½" down from bound off edge at each side of sleeve. Sew in sleeves, placing rows above markers between cast off sts at Front and Back armholes to form square armholes. Sew side and sleeve seams. Sew buttons on button band to correspond to buttonholes.

GIRL'S CARDIGAN
BACK

With smaller needles, cast on 75 {**93**-99} sts. Work 9 rows garter st, noting first row is **wrong side** and inc 20 sts evenly across last row. 95 {**113**-119} sts.

Change to larger needles and proceed in pat as follows:
1st and 3rd rows: (Right Side). Knit.
2nd and alt rows: K5 {**3**-6}. *P8. K3. Rep from * to last 2 {**0**-3} sts. K2 {**0**-3}.
5th row: K5 {**3**-6}. *C4B. C4F. K3. Rep from * to last 2 {**0**-3} sts. K2 {**0**-3}.
6th row: As 2nd row.
These 6 rows form pat.

Cont in pat until work from beg measures 8½ {**9½**-10½}", ending with right side facing for next row.

Armhole shaping: Keeping cont of pat, bind off 13 {**11**-14} sts beg of next 2 rows. 69 {**91**-91} sts.

Cont in pat until work from beg measures 15 {**16½**-18}", ending with right side facing for next row.

Next row: Bind off 19 {**29**-29} sts. Work pat across 31 {**33**-33} sts. Slip these 31 {**33**-33} sts onto a st holder. Bind off rem 19 {**29**-29} sts.

LEFT FRONT

With smaller needles, cast on 40 {**49**-52} sts. Work 9 rows garter st, inc 10 sts evenly across last row. 50 {**59**-62} sts.

Change to larger needles and proceed in pat as follows:
1st and 3rd rows: (Right Side). Knit.
2nd and alt rows: K4. *P8. K3. Rep from * to last 2 {**0**-3} sts. K2 {**0**-3}.
5th row: K5 {**3**-6}. *C4B. C4F. K3. Rep from * to last st. K1.
6th row: As 2nd row.
These 6 rows form pat.

Cont in pat until work from beg measures 8½ {**9½**-10½}", ending with right side facing for next row.

Armhole shaping: Keeping cont of pat, bind off 13 {**11**-14} sts beg of next row. 37 {**48**-48} sts.

Cont in pat until work from beg measures 12½ {**14**-15½}", ending with **wrong side** facing for next row.

Neck shaping: Next row: Bind off 10 sts (neck edge). Pat to end of row.
Keeping cont of pat, dec 1 st at neck edge on next 5 rows, then every alt row until there are 19 {**29**-29} sts.

Cont even until work from beg measures same length as Back to shoulder, ending with right side facing for next row. Bind off.

Place markers for five buttons along button band on Left Front, having top button ½" down from neck shaping and bottom button ½" above cast-on edge and rem 3 buttons spaced evenly between.

RIGHT FRONT

With smaller needles, cast on 40 {**49**-52} sts. Work 5 rows garter st.

Next row: (Buttonhole row). (Right Side). K2. Bind off 2 sts. Knit to end of row.

Next row: Knit, casting on 2 sts over bound off sts. Work a further 2 rows garter st, inc 10 sts evenly across last row. 50 {**59**-62} sts.

Note: Buttonholes are worked on Right Front to correspond to button markers on Left Front as follows:

Next row: (Right Side). K2. Bind off 2 sts. K1. Pat to end of row.

Next row: Work in pat, casting on 2 sts over bound off sts.

Change to larger needles and proceed in pat as follows:

1st and 3rd rows: (Right Side). Knit.

2nd and alt rows: K2 {**0**-3}. *K3. P8. Rep from * to last 4 sts. K4.

5th row: K4. *C4B. C4F. K3. Rep from * to last 2 {**0**-3} sts. K2 {**0**-3}.

6th row: As 2nd row.

These 6 rows form pat.

Cont in pat until work from beg measures 8½ {**9½**-10½}", ending with **wrong side** facing for next row.

Armhole shaping: Keeping cont of pat, cast off 13 {**11**-14} sts beg of next row. 37 {**48**-48} sts.

Cont in pat until work from beg measures 12½ {**14**-15½}", ending with right side facing for next row.

Neck shaping: Next row: Bind off 10 sts (neck edge). Pat to end of row.

Work 1 row even.

Keeping cont of pat, dec 1 st at neck edge on next 5 rows, then every alt row until there are 19 {**29**-29} sts.

Cont even until work from beg measures same length as Back to shoulder, ending with **wrong side** facing for next row. Bind off.

SLEEVES

With smaller needles, cast on 43 sts. Work 9 rows garter st, inc 15 sts evenly across last row. 58 sts.

Change to larger needles and proceed in pat as given for Back, inc 1 st at each end of needle on 3rd and every following alt row to 90 {**84**-88} sts then every following 4th row to 96 {**104**-108} sts, taking incs into pat until you have 7 complete cable reps, then taking inc sts into garter st.

Cont even until work from beg measures 11 {**11**-12}", ending with right side facing for next row.
Bind off in pat.

FINISHING

Pin garment pieces to measurements and cover with a damp cloth, leaving to dry.

Collar: Sew shoulder seams. With right side of work facing, smaller needles and beginning at center of button band, pick up and knit 18 {**19**-19} sts up Right Front neck edge. K23 {**25**-25} from Back st holder, dec 8 sts evenly across. Pick up and knit 18 {**19**-19} sts down Left Front neck edge, ending at center of buttonhole band. 59 {**63**-63} sts. Work garter st until Collar from beg measures 2", ending with **wrong side** facing for next row. Bind off.

Place markers 2" down from cast off edge at each side of sleeve. Sew in sleeves, placing rows above markers between bound off sts at Front and Back armholes to form square armholes. Sew side and sleeves seams. Sew buttons on button band to correspond to buttonholes.

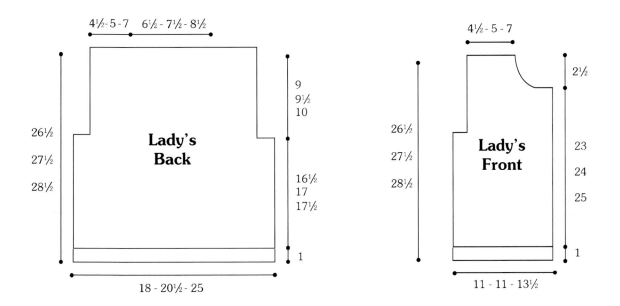

Lady's Back

4½ - 5 - 7   6½ - 7½ - 8½

9
9½
10

16½
17
17½

1

26½
27½
28½

18 - 20½ - 25

Lady's Front

4½ - 5 - 7

2½

23
24
25

1

26½
27½
28½

11 - 11 - 13½

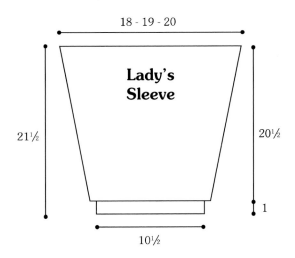

Lady's Sleeve

18 - 19 - 20

21½

20½

1

10½

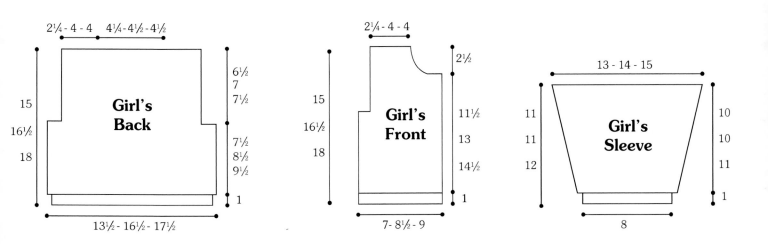

Girl's Back

2¼ - 4 - 4   4¼ - 4½ - 4½

6½
7
7½

7½
8½
9½

1

15
16½
18

13½ - 16½ - 17½

Girl's Front

2¼ - 4 - 4

2½

11½

13

14½

1

15
16½
18

7 - 8½ - 9

Girl's Sleeve

13 - 14 - 15

10

10

11

1

11
11
12

8

46

8. Utility Vest and Diamond Brights

Vest - Easy
Sweater - Intermediate

SIZES

UTILITY VEST

Bust/chest measurement

Small	34-36"
Medium	38-40"
Large	42-44"
Extra-Large	46-48"

Finished bust/chest

Small	41"
Medium	43½"
Large	48"
Extra-Large	51"

DIAMOND BRIGHTS

Chest measurement

4	23"
6	25"
8	26½"
10	28"

Finished chest

4	30½"
6	33"
8	36"
10	39"

Size Note: *Instructions for Lady's Utility Vest are written for size Small, with sizes Medium, Large, and Extra-Large in braces { }. Instructions for Girl's Diamond Brights are written for size 4, with sizes 6, 8, and 10 in braces { }. Instructions will be easier to read if you circle all the numbers pertaining to your size. If only one number is given, it applies to all sizes.*

MATERIALS

UTILITY VEST

Worsted Weight Yarn: 3½ oz (223 yds/100 g)

Sizes	S	M	L	XL	
Red	6	6	7	8	balls

Sample made with **Patons Classic Merino Wool.**

Size 11 (8 mm) knitting needles **or size needed for gauge.** 1 st holder. Separating zipper.

DIAMOND BRIGHTS

Worsted Weight Yarn: 3½ oz (223 yds/100 g)

Sizes	4	6	8	10	
Bright Green	1	2	2	2	ball(s)
Periwinkle	2	2	2	3	balls
Rust	1	1	1	2	ball(s)
Gold	1	1	2	2	ball(s)
Red	1	1	1	1	ball

Sample made with **Patons Classic Merino Wool.**

Sizes 5 (3.75 mm) and 7 (4.5 mm) knitting needles **or size needed for gauge.** 3 st holders. Zipper 6" long.

GAUGE SWATCH

UTILITY VEST: 11 sts and 16 rows = 4" with 2 strands of yarn in stocking st.
DIAMOND BRIGHTS: 20 sts and 26 rows = 4" with larger needles in stocking st.

UTILITY VEST

BACK

With 2 strands of yarn, cast on 51 {**55**-61-**65**} sts.
1st row: K1. *P1. K1. Rep from * to end of row.
2nd row: P1. *K1. P1. Rep from * to end of row.
Rep last 2 rows of (K1. P1) ribbing twice more and inc 5 sts evenly across last row. 56 {**60**-66-**70**} sts.

Beg with knit row, work in stocking st for 2", ending with right side facing for next row.
Proceed as follows:
**Next row: Purl.
Next row: Beg with purl row, cont in stocking st for 4", ending with right side facing for next row.**
Rep from ** to ** for pat until work from beg measures 16 {**16½**-17-**17½**}", ending with right side facing for next row.

Armhole shaping: Keeping cont of pat, bind off 3 sts beg next 2 rows. 50 {**54**-60-**74**} sts.
Dec 1 st at each end of needle on next and every alt row to 44 {**48**-54-**58**} sts.
Work even in pat until work from beg measures 25 {**26**-27-**28**}", ending with right side facing for next row.

Shoulder shaping: Bind off 6 {**6**-8-**8**} sts beg next 4 rows. Leave rem 20 {**22**-22-**26**} sts on a st holder.

RIGHT FRONT

***With 2 strands of yarn, cast on 25 {**27**-31-**33**} sts. Work 6 rows in (K1. P1) ribbing as given for Back and inc 3 sts evenly across last row. 28 {**30**-34-**36**} sts.
Beg with knit row, work in stocking st for 2", ending with right side facing for next row.***
Cont working in pat until work from beg measures 16 {**16½**-17-**17½**}", ending with **wrong side** facing for next row.

Armhole shaping: Keeping cont of pat, bind off 3 sts beg next row. 25 {**27**-31-**33**} sts.
Dec 1 st at armhole edge on next and every following alt row to 22 {**24**-28-**30**} sts.
Work even in pat until work from beg measures 22 {**23**-24-**25**}", ending with right side facing for next row.

Neck shaping: Bind off 5 {**6**-6-**7**} sts (neck edge). Pat to end of row.
Dec 1 st at neck edge on next 5 {**6**-6-**7**} rows. 12 {**12**-16-**16**} sts.

Cont even in pat until work from beg measures same length as Back to beg of shoulder shaping, ending with **wrong side** facing for next row.

Shoulder shaping: Bind off 6 {**6**-8-**8**} sts beg next row. Work 1 row even. Bind off rem 6 {**6**-8-**8**} sts.

LEFT FRONT

Work from *** to *** as given for Right Front.
Cont working in pat until work from beg measures 16 {**16½**-17-**17½**}", ending with right side facing for next row.

Armhole shaping: Keeping cont of pat, bind off 3 sts beg of next row. 25 {**27**-31-**33**} sts.
Work 1 row even.
Dec 1 st at armhole edge on next and every following alt row to 22 {**24**-28-**30**} sts.
Work even in pat until work from beg measures 22 {**23**-24-**25**}", ending with **wrong side** facing for next row.

Neck shaping: Bind off 5 {**6**-6-**7**} sts (neck edge). Pat to end of row.
Dec 1 st at neck edge on next 5 {**6**-6-**7**} rows to 12 {**12**-16-**16**} sts.
Cont even in pat until work from beg measures same length as Back to beg of shoulder shaping, ending with right facing for next row.

Shoulder shaping: Bind off 6 {**6**-8-**8**} sts beg next row. Work 1 row even. Bind off rem 6 {**6**-8-**8**} sts.

FINISHING

Pin garment pieces to measurements. Cover with a damp cloth leaving to dry.

Neckband: Sew shoulder seams. With right side of work facing and 2 strands of yarn, pick up and knit 15 {**16**-17-**18**} sts up Right Front neck edge. K20 {**22**-22-**26**} from Back st holder, dec 1 st at center. Pick up and knit 15 {**16**-17-**18**} sts down Left Front neck edge. 49 {**53**-55-**61**} sts.

Proceed as follows:
1st row: K1. *P1. K1. Rep from * to end of row.
2nd row: P1. *K1. P1. Rep from * to end of row.
Rep last 2 rows of (K1. P1) ribbing until neckband from pick up row measures 2", ending with right side facing for next row. Place marker at end of last row.

Break 1 strand of yarn. With 1 strand of yarn, work in stocking st for 2", ending with right side facing for next row. Bind off loosely.

Armbands: With right side of work facing and 2 strands of yarn, pick up and knit 30 {**32**-33-**35**} sts up armhole from side seam to shoulder seam. Pick up and knit 30 {**32**-33-**35**} sts down from shoulder seam to side seam. Work 3 rows in (K1. P1) ribbing as given for Back. Bind off in ribbing.

Zipper Edging: With right side of work facing and 2 strands of yarn, pick up and knit 66 {**69**-72-**74**} sts along Right Front from cast on edge to top of neckband marked row. Bind off. Rep for other side.

Right Pocket: With 2 strands of yarn, cast on 18 sts. Beg with knit row, work in stocking st until work from beg measures 2", ending with right side facing for next row.
Cont working in pat, as given for Back, for 2½", ending with **wrong side** facing for next row.
Next row: P2tog. Pat to end of row.
Next row: Work even in pat.
Rep last 2 rows to 11 sts then work even until pocket from beg measures 8", ending with right side facing for next row. Bind off.

Left Pocket: With 2 strands of yarn, cast on 18 sts. Beg with knit row, work in stocking st until work from beg measures 2", ending with right side facing for next row.
Cont working in pat, as given for Back, for 2½", ending with right side facing for next row.
Next row: Sl1. K1. psso. Pat to end of row.
Next row: Work even in pat.
Rep last 2 rows to 11 sts then work even until pocket from beg measures 8", ending with right side facing for next row. Bind off.

Sew side seams and armband seams. Fold neckband in half to **wrong side**, and pin in position.
Sew zipper in position, inserting between neckband layers and placing top of zipper at neckband marked row. Sew neckband seam loosely. Sew pockets in position, as shown in picture. **Do not press.**

DIAMOND BRIGHTS

Note: *When working from charts, carry yarn not in use loosely across wrong side of work but never over more than 5 sts. When it must pass over more than 5 sts, weave it over and under color in use on next st or at center point of sts it passes over. The colors are never twisted around one another.*

BACK
With smaller needles and Gold, cast on 74 {**78**-86-**94**} sts.

****1st row:** (Right Side). With Periwinkle, K2. *P2. K2. Rep from * to end of row.
2nd row: P2. *K2. P2. Rep from * to end of row.
Rep these 2 rows (K2. P2) ribbing for 1½", ending on a 2nd row and inc 2 {**4**-4-**4**} sts evenly across last row. 76 {**82**-90-**98**} sts.

Change to larger needles and work 2 rows in stocking st.
Next 2 rows: With Red, knit.
Work Chart II to end of chart, reading **knit** rows from **right** to **left** and **purl** rows from **left** to **right**, noting that 8 st rep will be worked 9 {**10**-11-**12**} times**. *Chart II is shown on page 52.*

*****Next 2 rows:** With Red, knit.
Work Chart III to end of chart, reading **knit** rows from **right** to left and **purl** rows from **left** to right, noting that 4 st rep will be worked 19 {**20**-22-**24**} times. *Chart III is shown on page 52.*

Next 2 rows: With Bright Green, purl.
With Rust, beg with a purl row, work 5 rows stocking st.
With Periwinkle, work 2 rows stocking st, ending with right side facing for next row.
Next 2 rows: With Gold, knit.
With Bright Green, work 6 rows stocking st, ending with right side facing for next row.
Work Chart IV to end of chart, reading **knit** rows from **right** to left and **purl** rows from **left** to right, noting that 2 st rep will be worked 38 {**41**-45-**49**} times. *Chart IV is shown on page 52.*

With Red, beg with a purl row, work 5 rows stocking st.
Next 2 rows: With Bright Green, knit.
With Gold, work 4 rows stocking st, ending with right side facing for next row.***

Work in Stripe Pat from *** to *** as given above, until work from beg measures 16 {17½-19½-20½}", ending with right side facing for next row.

Shoulder shaping: Cont working in Stripe Pat, bind off 12 {**13**-15-**17**} sts beg next 2 rows then 12 {**14**-15-**17**} sts beg following 2 rows. Leave rem 28 {**28**-30-**30**} sts on a st holder.

FRONT

Work from ** to ** as given for Back.
Work in Stripe Pat from *** to *** as given for Back, until work from beg measures 9½ {**10¾**-12¼-**13**}", ending with right side facing for next row.

Zipper opening: Next row: Work across 38 {**41**-45-**49**} sts (zipper opening). **Turn.** Leave rem sts on a spare needle.
Cont in Stripe Pat as established from *** to *** as given for Back, until zipper opening measures 4", ending with right side facing for next row.

Neck shaping: Next row: Pat to last 7 {**7**-8-**8**} sts (neck edge). **Turn.** Slip these 7 {**7**-8-**8**} sts onto a st holder. Dec 1 st at neck edge on next 4 rows, then every alt row to 24 {**27**-30-**34**} sts. Cont in Stripe Pat, until work from beg measures same length as Back before shoulder shaping, ending with right side facing for next row.

Shoulder shaping: Cont in Stripe Pat, bind off 12 {**13**-15-**17**} sts beg next row. Work 1 row even. Bind off rem 12 {**14**-15-**17**} sts.

With right side of work facing, join appropriate color to rem 38 {**41**-45-**49**} sts and pat to end of row.
With Periwinkle, work 1 {**1**-3-**3**} row(s) stocking st ending with right side facing for next row.

Next row: With Periwinkle, K10. Work 1st row of Chart V, reading row from **right** to left. With Periwinkle, K11 {**14**-18-**22**}.
Next row: With Periwinkle, P11 {**14**-18-**22**}. Work 2nd row of Chart V, reading row from **left** to right. With Periwinkle, P10.
Chart is now in position.

Cont working in Chart V until zipper opening measures 4", ending with **wrong side** facing for next row. *Chart V is shown on page 52.*

Neck shaping: Next row: Pat to last 7 {**7**-8-**8**} sts (neck edge). **Turn.** Slip these 7 {**7**-8-**8**} sts onto a st holder. Work 1 row even.
With Periwinkle, cont working in stocking st until Chart V is completed, dec 1 st at neck edge on next 4 rows, then every alt row to 24 {**27**-30-**34**} sts. Cont even until work from beg measures same length as Back before shoulder shaping, ending with **wrong side** facing for next row.

Shoulder shaping: Bind off 12 {**13**-15-**17**} sts beg next row. Work 1 row even. Bind off rem 12 {**14**-15-**17**} sts.

SLEEVES

With smaller needles and Gold, cast on 38 {**38**-46-**46**} sts.
With Periwinkle, work in (K2. P2) ribbing as given for Back for 1½", ending on a 2nd row.

Change to larger needles and work 2 rows in stocking st, ending with right side facing for next row.
Next row: With Red, inc 1 st in first st. Knit to last 2 sts. Inc 1 st in next st. K1.
Next row: With Red, knit. 40 {**40**-48-**48**} sts.
Work Chart VI to end of chart, noting that 8 st rep will be worked 5 {**5**-5-**6**} times and inc 1 st each end of needle on every 2nd row from previous inc 9 times. *Chart VI is shown on page 52.*

Work from *** to *** as given for Back, inc 1 st each end of needle on every 4th row to 70 {**78**-86-**88**} sts. Cont even in Stripe Pat until work from beg measures 10½ {**12**-13½-**15**}", ending with right side facing for next row. Bind off.

FINISHING

Pin all garment pieces to measurements. Cover with a damp cloth leaving to dry.

Collar: Sew shoulder seams. With right side of work facing, smaller needles and Periwinkle, K7 {**7**-8-**8**} from Right Front st holder. Pick up and knit 14 {**14**-16-**18**} sts up Right Front neck edge. K28 {**28**-30-**30**} from Back neck st holder. Pick up and knit 14 {**14**-16-**18**} sts down Left Front neck edge. K7 {**7**-8-**8**} from Left Front st holder. 70 {**70**-78-**82**} sts.
Beg with a 2nd row, work in (K2. P2) ribbing as given for Back for 2", ending with right side facing for next row. With Gold, rib 1 row. Bind off in ribbing.

Zipper Edging: With right side of work facing, smaller needles and Gold, pick up and knit 30 sts down Left Front zipper opening from bound off edge of collar. Pick up 1 st at turning point. Pick up and knit 30 sts up Right Front zipper opening to bound off edge. 61 sts. Bind off knitwise (**wrong side**).

Sew zipper in position under zipper edging.
Place markers on Front and Back side edges 7 {7¾-8½-8¾}" down from shoulder seams. Sew in sleeves between markers. Sew side and sleeve seams. **Do not press.**

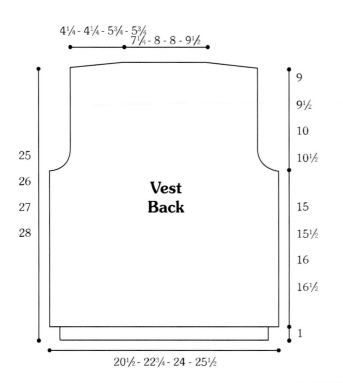

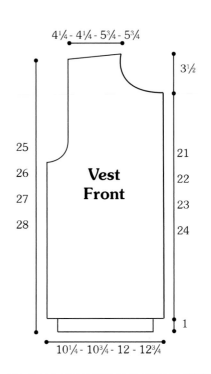

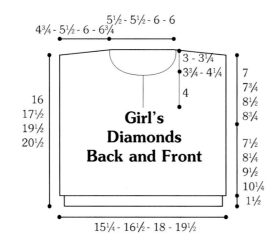

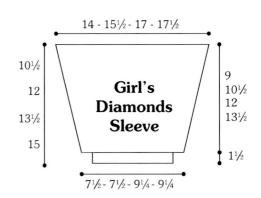

Chart II

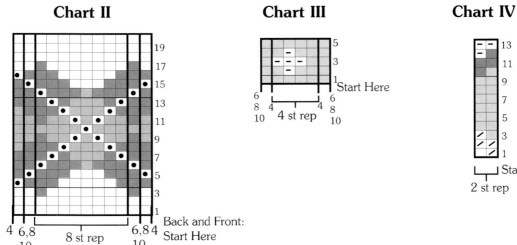

Back and Front:
Start Here

4 6,8   8 st rep   6,8 4
   10   10

Chart III

Start Here
6   6
8   8
10 4 st rep 10

Chart IV

Start Here
2 st rep

Chart V

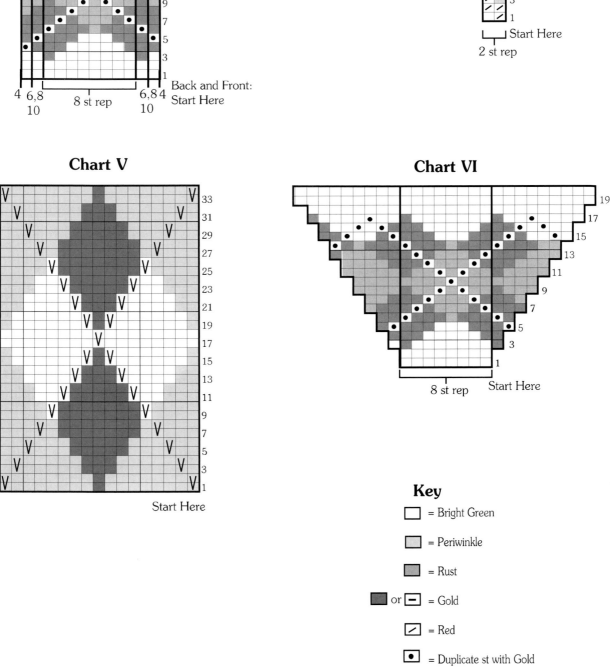

Start Here

Chart VI

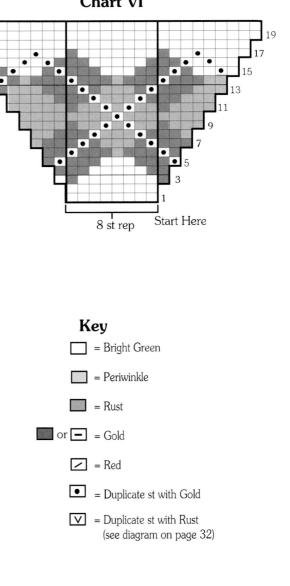

8 st rep   Start Here

Key

☐ = Bright Green

☐ = Periwinkle

☐ = Rust

☐ or ⊟ = Gold

⟋ = Red

⊡ = Duplicate st with Gold

Ⅴ = Duplicate st with Rust
(see diagram on page 32)

9. Big-Stitch Pullovers

Easy

Sizes

HIS & HERS
Bust/chest measurement

Small	30-32"
Medium	34-36"
Large	38-40"
Extra-Large	42-44"

Finished bust/chest

Small	39"
Medium	43½"
Large	48"
Extra-Large	52"

KID'S
Chest measurement

4	23"
6	25"
8	26½"
10	28"

Finished chest

4	29"
6	32"
8	33½"
10	39"

Size Note: Adult instructions are written for size Small, with sizes Medium, Large, and Extra-Large in braces { }. Kid's instructions are written for size 4, with sizes 6, 8, and 10 in braces { }. Instructions will be easier to read if you circle all the numbers pertaining to your size. If only one number is given, it applies to all sizes.

MATERIALS

Worsted Weight Yarn: 3½ oz (223 yds/100 g)

HER VERSION

Sizes	S	M	L	XL	
Periwinkle	6	7	8	9	balls
Variegated	1	2	2	2	ball(s)

HIS VERSION

Sizes	S	M	L	XL	
Navy	7	8	8	9	balls

KID'S VERSION

Sizes	4	6	8	10	
Variegated	4	4	6	6	balls

Samples made with **Patons Classic Merino Wool.**

Size 11 (8 mm) knitting needles **or size needed for gauge.** 2 st holders.

GAUGE SWATCH

11 sts and 16 rows = 4" with 2 strands of yarn in stocking st.

HIS & HERS VERSION
BACK
With 2 strands of Periwinkle (for Her) or Navy (for Him), cast on 53 {59**-**65**-**71**} sts.
1st row: (Right Side). K2. *P1. K2. Rep from * to end of row.
2nd row: P2. *K1. P2. Rep from * to end of row. Rep these 2 rows (K2. P1) ribbing for 2", ending on a 2nd row and inc 1 st at center of last row. 54 {**60**-66-**72**} sts.

His Version only: Proceed in stocking st until work from beg measures 16 {**16½-16¾-17**}", ending with right side facing for next row.

Her Version only: Work 4 rows stocking st.
Next 2 rows: With one strand of Periwinkle and one strand of Variegated, work 2 rows stocking st.
Last 6 rows form pat.
Cont in pat until work from beg measures 16 {**16½-16¾-17**}", ending with right side facing for next row.

Both Versions: Armhole shaping: Bind off 2 sts beg next 2 rows.**
Cont in stocking st until work from beg measures 25 {**26-27-28**}", ending with right side facing for next row.

Shoulder shaping: Bind off 5 {**6-6-7**} sts beg next 2 rows, then 5 {**6-7-8**} sts beg next 4 rows. Leave rem 20 {**20-22-22**} sts on a st holder.

FRONT
Work from ** to ** as given for Back.
Cont in pat for Her Version and in stocking st for His Version until work from beg measures 22 {**23-23½-24½**}", ending with right side facing for next row.

Neck shaping: Next row: K22 {**25-28-31**} (neck edge). **Turn.** Leave rem sts on a spare needle.
Dec 1 st at neck edge on next 7 {**7-8-8**} rows. 15 {**18-20-23**} sts.
Cont even until work from beg measures 25 {**26-27-28**}", ending with right side facing for next row.

Shoulder shaping: Bind off 5 {**6-6-7**} sts beg next row. Work 1 row even. Bind off 5 {**6-7-8**} sts on next and following alt row.

With right side of work facing, slip next 6 sts from spare needle onto a st holder. Join 2 strands of yarn to rem sts and knit to end of row.
Dec 1 st at neck edge on next 7 {**7-8-8**} rows. 15 {**18-20-23**} sts. Cont even until work from beg measures 25 {**26-27-28**}", ending with **wrong side** facing for next row.

Shoulder shaping: Bind off 5 {**6-6-7**} sts beg next row. Work 1 row even. Bind off 5 {**6-7-8**} sts on next and following alt row.

SLEEVES
With 2 strands of Periwinkle (for Her) or Navy (for Him), cast on 20 {**20-26-26**} sts.
Work in (K2. P1) ribbing, as given for Back and inc 2 {**2-0-0**} sts evenly across last row. 22 {**22-26-26**} sts.

Cont working in pat for Her Version and in stocking st for His Version, inc 1 st each end of needle on 3rd and every following 4th row to 46 {**48-48-58**} sts, then every following 6th row to 50 {**52-56-60**} sts. Cont even until work from beg measures 17½ {**18-19-19½**}", ending with right side facing for next row. Bind off.

FINISHING
Pin garment pieces to measurements. Cover with a damp cloth, leaving to dry.

Neckband: Sew right shoulder seam. With right side of work facing and 2 strands of Periwinkle (for Her) or Navy (for Him), pick up and knit 12 {**12-15-15**} sts down Left Front neck edge. K6 from Front neck st holder. Pick up and knit 12 {**12-15-15**} up Right Front neck edge. K20 {**20-22-22**} from Back neck st holder, dec 0 {**0-2-2**} sts evenly across. 50 {**50-56-56**} sts.

Her Version only: Beg with a 2nd row, work in (K2. P1) ribbing for 4", as given for Back, ending with right side facing for next row. Bind off.
Sew left shoulder and neckband seam. Sew in sleeves. Sew side and sleeve seams. **Do not press.**

His Version only: Beg with a 2nd row, work in (K2. P1) ribbing for 3", as given for Back, ending with right side facing for next row. Bind off loosely.

Sew left shoulder and neckband seam. Fold neckband in half to **wrong side** and sew loosely in position. Sew in sleeves. Sew side and sleeve seams.
Do not press.

KID'S VERSION
BACK
With 2 stands of yarn, cast on 38 {41-44-47**} sts.
1st row: (Right Side). K2. *P1. K2. Rep from * to end of row.
2nd row: P2. *K1. P2. Rep from * to end of row.
Rep these 2 rows (K2. P1) ribbing for 2", ending on

a 2nd row and inc 2 {**3**-2-**3**} sts evenly across last row. 40 {**44**-46-**50**} sts.

Proceed in stocking st until work from beg measures 10 {**11½**-13-**13½**}", ending with right side facing for next row.

Armhole shaping: Bind off 2 sts beg next 2 rows. 36 {**40**-42-**46**} sts.**

Cont in stocking st until work from beg measures 17 {**19**-21-**22**}", ending with right side facing for next row.

Shoulder shaping: Bind off 4 {**5**-5-**6**} sts beg next 2 rows then 5 {**6**-6-**7**} sts beg following 2 rows. Leave rem 18 {**18**-20-**20**} sts on a st holder.

FRONT

Work from ** to ** as given for Back.

Cont in stocking st until work from beg measures 14 {**16**-18-**19**}", ending with right side facing for next row.

Neck shaping: Next row: K15 {**17**-18-**20**} (neck edge). **Turn.** Leave rem sts on spare needle.

Dec 1 st at neck edge on next 6 {**6**-7-**7**} rows. 9 {**11**-11-**13**} sts.

Cont even in stocking st until work from beg measures 18 {**20**-22-**24**}", ending with right side facing for next row.

Shoulder shaping: Bind off 4 {**5**-5-**6**} sts beg next row. Work 1 row even. Bind off rem 5 {**6**-6-**7**} sts.

With right side of work facing, slip next 6 sts from spare needle onto a st holder. Join yarn to rem sts and knit to end of row.

Dec 1 st at neck edge on next 6 {**6**-7-**7**} rows. 9 {**11**-11-**13**} sts.

Cont even in stocking st until work from beg measures 17 {**19**-21-**22**}", ending with **wrong side** facing for next row.

Shoulder shaping: Bind off 4 {**5**-5-**6**} sts beg next row. Work 1 row even. Bind off rem 5 {**6**-6-**7**} sts.

SLEEVES

With 2 strands of yarn, cast on 23 sts.

Work in (K2. P1) ribbing as given for Back for 2" ending on a 2nd row.

Cont in stocking st, inc 1 st each end of needle on 3rd and every following 4th row to 39 {**41**-45-**47**} sts.

Cont even in stocking st until work from beg measures 11½ {**13**-15-**15½**}", ending with right side facing for next row. Bind off.

FINISHING

Pin garment pieces to measurements. Cover with a damp cloth, leaving to dry.

Neckband: Sew right shoulder seam. With right side of work facing and 2 strands of yarn, pick up and knit 9 {**9**-12-**12**} sts down Left Front neck edge. K6 from Front st holder. Pick up and knit 9 {**9**-12-**12**} sts up Right Front neck edge. K18 {**18**-20-**20**} from Back st holder. 42 {**42**-50-**50**} sts.

Next row: Beg with a purl row, work in stocking st for 2", ending with right side facing for next row. Bind off.

Sew left shoulder and neckband seam, reversing seam for turn-back. Sew in sleeves. Sew side and sleeve seams.

Do not press.

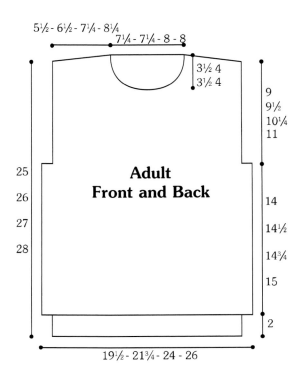

5½ - 6½ - 7¼ - 8¼

7¼ - 7¼ - 8 - 8

3½ 4
3½ 4

9
9½
10¼
11

25

26

27

28

**Adult
Front and Back**

14

14½

14¾

15

2

19½ - 21¾ - 24 - 26

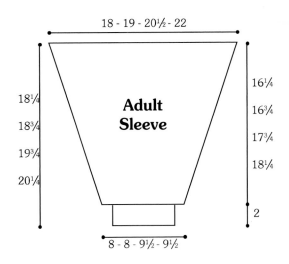

18 - 19 - 20½ - 22

18¼

18¾

19¾

20¼

**Adult
Sleeve**

16¼

16¾

17¾

18¼

2

8 - 8 - 9½ - 9½

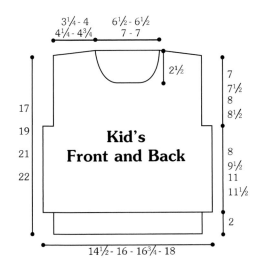

3¼ - 4
4¼ - 4¾

6½ - 6½
7 - 7

2½

7
7½
8
8½

17

19

21

22

**Kid's
Front and Back**

8
9½
11
11½

2

14½ - 16 - 16¾ - 18

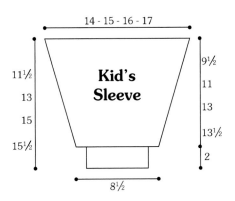

14 - 15 - 16 - 17

11½

13

15

15½

**Kid's
Sleeve**

9½

11

13

13½

2

8½

10. Like Father Like Son

Intermediate

SIZES

To fit Child 4-6 yrs/Adult.

Size Note: Instructions are written for Child's size, with Adult's size in braces { }. Instructions will be easier to read if you circle all the numbers pertaining to your size. If only one number is given, it applies to all sizes.

MATERIALS

Worsted Weight Yarn: 3½ oz (223 yds/100 g)

Sizes	Child	Adult	
Ear Flap Version or Plain Version Hat			
Beige	1	1	ball
Grey	1	1	ball
Black	1	1	ball
Mittens			
Black	1	1	ball
Small amount of Grey			

Samples made with **Patons Classic Merino Wool.**

Sizes 5 (3.75 mm) and 7 (4.5 mm) knitting needles **or size needed for gauge.** Size 5 (3.75 mm) circular knitting needle 24" long for Ear Flap Version Hat.

GAUGE SWATCH

Hat: 20 sts and 26 rows = 4" with larger needles in stocking st.
Mittens: 21 sts and 28 rows = 4" with smaller needles in stocking st.

STITCH GUIDE

M1 = make one st by picking up horizontal loop lying before next st and knitting into back of loop.
M1P = make one st by picking up horizontal loop lying before next st and purling into back of loop.

EAR FLAP VERSION HAT

Ear Flap: (make 2). With Beige and larger needles cast on 13 sts.
1st row: (Right Side). Knit.
2nd row: P1. M1P. Purl to last st. M1P. P1.
3rd row: K1. M1. Knit to last st. M1. K1.
4th row: As 2nd row. 19 sts.

5th row: K1. M1. K1. Work 1st row of Chart VII across next 15 sts. K1. M1. K1.
6th row: P1. M1P. P2. Work 2nd row of Chart VII across next 15 sts. P2. M1P. P1. 23 sts.
Chart VII is now in position. *Chart VII is shown on page 59.*

Cont even, working Chart VII to end of chart. Break Grey.
With Beige, work 3 rows even in stocking st thus ending with right side facing for next row. Break yarn. Leave sts on a spare needle.

Body of Hat: With Beige and larger needles, cast on 6 {**9**} sts. Knit these sts and 23 sts of first Ear Flap. **Turn** and cast on 36 {**44**} sts. **Turn** and K23 of second Ear Flap. **Turn** and cast on 6 {**9**} sts. 94 {**108**} sts.
Next row: Purl.
Work Chart VIII to end of chart noting the 7 st rep will be worked 13 {15**} times. *Chart VIII is shown on page 59.*
Next row: (Right Side). *With Beige, K9 {**11**}. K2tog. Rep from * 7 times more. K6 {**4**}. 86 {**100**} sts.
Next row: Purl.
Next row: *K12 {**23**}. K2tog. Rep from * 5 {**3**} times more. K2 {**0**}. 80 {**96**} sts.

Next row: Purl.

Work Chart IX to end of chart noting the 16 st rep will be worked 5 (**6**) times. Break Beige. *Chart IX is shown on page 59.*

Top shaping: 1st row: (Right Side). With Black, knit, dec 2 sts evenly across. 78 {**94**} sts.

2nd and alt rows: Purl.

3rd row: K2. Sl1. K1. psso. *K13 {**17**}. K2tog. K2. Sl1. K1. psso. Rep from * twice more. K13 {**17**}. K2tog. K2. 70 {**86**} sts.

5th row: K2. Sl1. K1. psso. *K11 {**15**}. K2tog. K2. Sl1. K1. psso. Rep from * twice more. K11 {**15**}. K2tog. K2. 62 {**78**} sts.

7th row: K2. Sl1. K1. psso. *K9 {**13**}. K2tog. K2. Sl1. K1. psso. Rep from * twice more. K9 {**13**}. K2tog. K2. 54 {**70**} sts.

8th row: Purl.

Cont in this manner, dec 8 sts evenly across next and every following alt row until there are 30 sts.

Next row: K2. Sl1. K1. psso. *K1. K2tog. K2. Sl1. K1. psso. Rep from * twice more. K1. K2tog. K2. 22 sts.

Next row: P2. *P2tog. P2. Rep from * to end of row. 17 sts.

Next row: K1. (K2tog) 8 times. 9 sts.

Work 5 rows even. Break yarn leaving a long end. Draw end through rem sts and fasten securely.**

Edging: With right side of work facing, Beige and circular needle, pick up and knit 6 {**9**} sts along center Back cast on sts, 53 sts around Ear Flap, 32 {**40**} sts across center Front cast on sts, 53 sts around 2nd Ear Flap and 6 {**9**} sts along rem center Back cast on sts. 150 {**164**} sts. **Do not** join.

Working back and forth across needle in rows, proceed as follows:

Knit 2 rows. Bind off knitwise (**wrong side**). Sew center back seam.

PLAIN VERSION HAT

With Beige and smaller needles, cast on 94 {**108**} sts. Work 5 rows garter st (knit every row), noting that 1st row is **wrong side**.

Next row: (Right Side). Knit.

Next row: Purl.

Change to larger needles and work as given for Ear Flap Version from ** to **. Sew center back seam.

MITTENS

Right Mitten: **With Black and smaller needles, cast on 36 {**44**} sts.

1st row: (Right Side). *K2. P2. Rep from * to end of row. This row forms (K2. P2) ribbing.

Work a further 17 {**21**} rows in (K2. P2) ribbing.

Work 6 {**10**} rows stocking st.**

Shape thumb gusset: 1st row: K19 {**23**}. Inc 1 st in each of next 2 sts. Knit to end of row.

2nd and alt rows: Purl.

3rd row: K19 {**23**}. Inc 1 st in next st. K2. Inc 1 st in next st. Knit to end of row.

5th row: K19 {**23**}. Inc 1 st in next st. K4. Inc 1 st in next st. Knit to end of row.

6th row: Purl.

Cont in this manner having 2 sts more between incs for thumb gusset every alt row until there are 46 {**56**} sts.

Next row: Purl.

Make thumb: Next row: K31 {**37**}. **Turn.** Cast on 1 st. P12 {**14**} (including cast on st). **Turn.** Cast on 1 st. Working on these 13 {**15**} sts, cont even in stocking st for 1¾ {**2½**}", ending with right side facing for next row.

Next row: K1. *K2tog. Rep from * to end of row. 6 {**8**} sts. Break yarn leaving a long end. Draw end through rem sts and fasten securely. Sew thumb seam.

Remainder of Mitten: With right side of work facing, join Black to last st on right-hand needle. Pick up and knit 2 sts at base of thumb. Knit across sts on left-hand needle.

Next row: Purl, working P2tog over picked up sts at base of thumb. 36 {**44**} sts.
Cont even until work after ribbing measures 4¾ {**6½**}", ending with right side facing for next row.

Shape top: 1st row: K1. Sl1. K1. psso. K12 {**16**}. K2tog. K2. Sl1. K1. psso. Knit to last 3 sts. K2tog. K1.
2nd and alt rows: Purl.
3rd row: K1. Sl1. K1. psso. K10 {**14**}. K2tog. K2. Sl1. K1. psso. Knit to last 3 sts. K2tog. K1.
5th row: K1. Sl1. K1. psso. K8 {**12**}. K2tog. K2. Sl1. K1. psso. Knit to last 3 sts. K2tog. K1.
6th row: Purl.
Cont in this manner, having 2 sts fewer between decs on next and every following alt row until there are 20 sts. Bind off purlwise.

Work Chart VII in duplicate st on center of Mitten as illustrated below. Sew top and side seam.

Left Mitten: Work from ** to ** as given for Right Mitten.

Shape thumb gusset: 1st row: K14 {**18**}. Inc 1 st in each of next 2 sts. Knit to end of row.
2nd and alt rows: Purl.
3rd row: K14 {**18**}. Inc 1 st in next st. K2. Inc 1 st in next st. Knit to end of row.
5th row: K14 {**18**}. Inc 1 st in next st. K4. Inc 1 st in next st. Knit to end of row.
6th row: Purl.
Cont in this manner, having 2 sts more between incs for thumb gusset every alt row until there are 46 {**56**} sts.
Next row: Purl.

Make thumb: Next row: K26 {**32**}. **Turn.** Cast on 1 st. P12 {**14**} (including cast on st). **Turn.** Cast on 1 st. Working on these 13 {**15**} sts, cont even in stocking st for 1¾ {**2½**}", ending with right side facing for next row.
Next row: K1. *K2tog. Rep from * to end of row. 6 {**8**} sts. Break yarn leaving a long end. Draw end through rem sts and fasten securely. Sew thumb seam.

Remainder of Mitten: Work as given for Right Mitten.

DUPLICATE STITCH

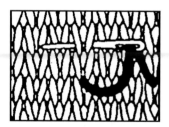

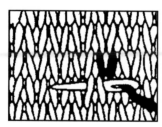

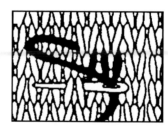

Bring needle up through centre of stitch from back of work and * insert from right to left behind stitch immediately above.

Bring needle down through center of original stitch and out through center of next stitch to be worked.

Repeat from * to continue.

Chart VII

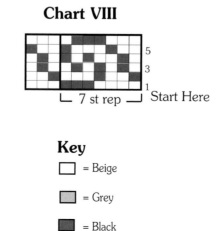

Start Here

Chart VIII

└ 7 st rep ┘ Start Here

Key

☐ = Beige

▨ = Grey

■ = Black

Chart IX

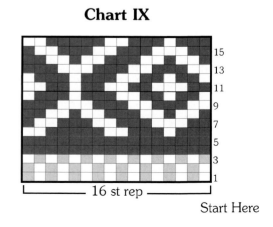

└─── 16 st rep ───┘

Start Here

59

11. Cable Hats & Bags

Intermediate

SIZES

Hat: To fit Child 4-6 yrs/Average Lady.

Size Note: Instructions are written for Child's size, with Adult's size in braces { }. Instructions will be easier to read if you circle all the numbers pertaining to your size. If only one number is given, it applies to all sizes.

MATERIALS

Worsted Weight Yarn: 3½ oz (201 yds/100 g)

Lady's Version
Hat: Red	1	**ball**
Bag: Red	2	**balls**

Girl's Version
Hat: Orange	1	**ball**
Bag: Orange	1	**ball**

Samples made with **Patons Classic Merino Wool.**

Size 7 (4.5 mm) knitting needles **or size needed for gauge.** Cable needle.

GAUGE SWATCH

20 sts and 26 rows = 4" in stocking st.

STITCH GUIDE

C4F = slip next 2 sts onto a cable needle and leave at front of work. K2, then K2 from cable needle.
Sl1P = slip next st purlwise.
yf = take yarn to front of work.
yb = take yarn to back of work.

Panel Pat
1st row: (Right Side). P1. K2tog. yo. *P2. K4. P2. K2tog. yo. Rep from * to last st. P1.
2nd and alt rows: K1. P2. *K2. P4. K2. P2. Rep from * to last st. K1.
3rd row: P1. yo. Sl1. K1. psso. *P2. K4. P2. yo. Sl1. K1. psso. Rep from * to last st. P1.
5th row: As 1st row.
7th row: P1. yo. Sl1. K1. psso. *P2. C4F. P2. yo. Sl1. K1. psso. Rep from * to last st. P1.
8th row: As 2nd row.
These 8 rows form Panel Pat.

HAT

Cast on 90 {**96**} sts.
Work 5 rows stocking st.
Next row: (**Wrong Side**). Knit, inc 14 {**18**} sts evenly across. 104 {**114**} sts.
Work 1st to 8th rows of Panel Pat 5 times.

Lady's Version only: Work 1st to 4th rows of Panel Pat once.

All Sizes: Next row: (Right Side). P1. K2tog. yo. *P2. K1. K2tog. K1. P2. K2tog. yo. Rep from * to last st. P1. 94 {**103**} sts.
Next row: K1. P2. *K2. P3. K2. P2. Rep from * to last st. K1.
Next row: P1. yo. Sl1. K1. psso. *P2. K1. K2tog. P2. yo. Sl1. K1. psso. Rep from * to last st. P1. 84 {**92**} sts.
Next row: Knit.
Next row: (Eyelet row). *K2tog. yo. K2. Rep from * to end of row.

Next row: Knit.
Next row: P1. *K2. P2. Rep from * to last 3 sts. K2. P1.
Next row: K1. *P2. K2. Rep from * to last 3 sts. P2. K1.
Rep last 2 rows twice more, dec 20 {**22**} sts evenly across last row. 64 {**70**} sts.
Work 4 rows in stocking st. Bind off.

FINISHING

Sew back seam of Hat, reversing seam at rolled edges.

Twisted cord: Cut 2 strands of yarn 54" long. With both strands tog hold one end and with someone holding other end, twist strands to the right until they begin to curl. Fold the 2 ends tog and tie in a knot so they will not unravel. The strands will now twist themselves tog. Adjust length if desired. Weave cord through eyelet row and tie.

Tassel: (Make 2). Cut a piece of cardboard 2" wide. Wind yarn around cardboard 25 times. Break yarn leaving a long end and thread end through a needle. Slip needle through all loops and tie tightly. Remove cardboard and wind yarn tightly around loops ¾" below fold. Fasten securely. Cut through rem loops and trim ends evenly. Attach tassel to each end of twisted cord.

LADY'S BAG

Cast on 102 sts.
Work 4 rows in stocking st, inc 22 sts evenly across last row. 124 sts.
Work 1st to 7th rows of Panel Pat.
Next row: (**Wrong Side**). Knit.
Next row: (Eyelet row). *K2tog. yo. K2. Rep from * to end of row.
Next row: Knit.
Work 1st to 8th rows of Panel Pat 5 times, then 1st to 7th rows once.
Next row: Purl, dec 22 sts evenly across. 102 sts. Place first set of markers at each end of row.
Work 4 rows in stocking st. Place second set of markers at each end of last row.

Shape bottom: 1st row: (Right Side). K2. *K2tog. K8. Rep from * to end of row. 92 sts.
2nd and alt rows: Purl.
3rd row: K2. *K2tog. K7. Rep from * to end of row. 82 sts.
5th row: K2. *K2tog. K6. Rep from * to end of row. 72 sts.
Cont in this manner, dec 10 sts every alt row, until there are 12 sts. Break yarn leaving a long end. Draw yarn through rem sts. Fasten securely.

With **wrong side** of work facing, sew marked rows tog to form ridge.

Strap: Cast on 6 sts.
1st row: (Right Side). (K1. yf. Sl1P. yb) twice. K2.
2nd row: (P1. yb. Sl1P. yf) twice. P2.
Rep last 2 rows until work from beg measures 40" (or desired length), ending with right side facing for next row. Bind off. Attach each end to inside of Bag below eyelet row.

Twisted cord: Cut 2 strands of yarn 60" long. With both strands tog make twisted cord as given for Hat. Adjust length if desired. Thread cord through eyelet row and tie. Make 2 tassels as given for Hat and secure to each end of cord.

GIRL'S BAG (make 2 pieces alike)

Cast on 37 sts.
Work 5 rows in garter st (knit every row), noting that first row is **wrong side** and inc 3 sts evenly across last row. 40 sts.
Proceed in stocking st until work from beg measures 10", ending with right side facing for next row. 37 sts.
Bind off.

Pocket

Cast on 34 sts.
Proceed in Panel Pat until work from beg measures 2½", ending with right side facing for next row.

Pocket shaping: 1st row: Pat 3 sts. Work 2tog. Pat to last 5 sts. Work 2tog. Pat 3 sts.
2nd row: Knit all knit sts and purl all purl sts as they appear.
Rep last 2 rows to 18 sts, ending with right side facing for next row. Bind off in pat.

FINISHING

Sew pocket to front of Bag as illustrated leaving shaped sides open. Sew side and bottom seams of Bag.

Twisted cord: Cut 4 strands of yarn 100" long. With all strands tog make twisted cord as given for Hat. Adjust length if desired.
Sew ends of twisted cord inside top edge of Bag.
Make 2 tassels as given for Hat.
Sew 1 tassel to each lower corner of Bag as shown in picture.

11

16

12. Pretty Lace Cardigans

Advanced

SIZES
WOMAN'S VERSION
To fit bust measurement

Small	34"
Medium	36"
Large	38"
Extra-Large	40"

Finished bust

Small	39"
Medium	41½"
Large	44"
Extra-Large	47"

GIRL'S VERSION
To fit chest measurement

4	23"
6	25"
8	26½"

Finished chest

4	28"
6	31"
8	33½"

Size Note: Instructions for Woman's Cardigan are written for size Small, with sizes Medium, Large, and Extra-Large in braces { }. Instructions for Girl's Cardigan are written for size 4, with sizes 6 and 8 in braces. { }. Instructions will be easier to read if you circle all the numbers pertaining to your size. If only one number is given, it applies to all sizes.

MATERIALS

Sport Weight Yarn: 1¾ oz (133 yds/50 g)

Woman's Version

Sizes	S	M	L	XL	
Pale Green	8	8	9	10	balls

Girl's Version

Sizes	4	6	8	
Light Blue	5	5	6	balls

Samples made with **Patons Astra.**

Sizes 5 (3.75 mm) and 6 (4 mm) knitting needles. Size 5 (3.75 mm) circular knitting needle **or size needed for gauge.** St holder. 7 buttons for Woman's Version. 5 buttons for Girl's Version.

GAUGE SWATCH
21 sts and 34 rows = 4" with larger needles in Lace Pat.

WOMAN'S VERSION
BACK
With smaller needles, cast on 99 (**106**-113-**120**} sts.
1st row: (Right Side). P1. *P1. K2. yo. Sl1. K1. psso. P2. Rep from * to end of row.
2nd row: *K2. P4. K1. Rep from * to last st. K1.
3rd row: P1. *P1. K2tog. yo. K2. P2. Rep from * to end of row.
4th row: As 2nd row.
These 4 rows form Eyelet Rib Pat.
Work a further 8 rows in Eyelet Rib Pat, inc 3 sts evenly across last row. 102 {**109**-116-**123**} sts.

Change to larger needles and proceed in Lace Pat as follows: (*See Chart on page 74.*)

1st row: (Right Side). K3. *Sl1. K1. psso. K5. yo. Rep from * to last st. K1.

2nd and alt rows: Purl.

3rd row: K3. *Sl1. K1. psso. K4. yo. K1. Rep from * to last st. K1.

5th row: K3. *Sl1. K1. psso. K3. yo. K2. Rep from * to last st. K1.

7th row: K3. *Sl1. K1. psso. K2. yo. K3. Rep from * to last st. K1.

9th row: K3. *Sl1. K1. psso. K1. yo. K4. Rep from * to last st. K1.

11th row: K3. *Sl1. K1. psso. yo. K5. Rep from * to last st. K1.

13th row: K1. *yo. K5. K2tog. Rep from * to last 3 sts. K3.

15th row: K2. *yo. K4. K2tog. K1. Rep from * to last 2 sts. K2.

17th row: K3. *yo. K3. K2tog. K2. Rep from * to last st. K1.

19th row: K4. *yo. K2. K2tog. K3. Rep from * to end of row.

21st row: K5. *yo. K1. K2tog. K4. Rep from * to last 6 sts. yo. K1. K2tog. K3.

23rd row: K6. *yo. K2tog. K5. Rep from * to last 5 sts. yo. K2tog. K3.

24th row: Purl.

These 24 rows form Lace Pat.

Cont in Lace Pat until work from beg measures approx 12", ending on a 16th row of Lace Pat.

Armhole shaping: 1st row: (Right Side). Bind off 3 sts (1 st rem after bind off). yo. K2. K2tog. K2. *yo. K3. K2tog. K2. Rep from * to last st. K1.

2nd row: Bind off 3 sts. Purl to end of row.

3rd row: Sl1. K1. psso. yo. K1. K2tog. K3. *yo. K2. K2tog. K3. Rep from * to last 4 sts. yo. K2. K2tog.

4th row: P2tog. Purl to end of row.

5th row: Sl1. K1. psso. K6. *yo. K1. K2tog. K4. Rep from * to last 2 sts. K2tog.

6th row: Purl.

7th row: Sl1. K1. psso. K6. *yo. K2tog. K5. Rep from * to last 7 sts. yo. K2tog. K3. K2tog.

8th row: P2tog. Purl to last 2 sts. P2togtbl. 88 {**95**-102-**109**} sts.

Beg with 1st row of Lace Pat, cont even in pat until armhole measures approx 7 {**7½**-8-**8½**}", ending on a 10th {**12th**-14th-**18th**} row.

Shoulder shaping: Bind off 13 {**14**-15-**17**} sts beg next 2 rows, then bind off 13 {**15**-16-**17**} sts beg following 2 rows. Leave rem 36 {**37**-40-**41**} sts on a st holder.

LEFT FRONT

With smaller needles, cast on 50 {57**-57-**64**} sts. Work 12 rows in Eyelet Rib Pat as given for Back, inc 3 sts evenly across last row. 53 {**60**-60-**67**} sts.

Change to larger needles and proceed in Lace Pat as given for Back until work from beg measures approx 12", ending on a 16th row of Lace Pat.**

Armhole and V-neck shaping: 1st row: (Right Side). Bind off 3 sts (1 st rem on needle after bind off). yo. K2. K2tog. K2. *yo. K3. K2tog. K2. Rep from * to last 8 sts. yo. K3. K2tog. K1. K2tog.

2nd row: Purl.

3rd row: Sl1. K1. psso. yo. K1. K2tog. K3. *yo. K2. K2tog. K3. Rep from * to last 6 sts. yo. K2. (K2tog) twice.

4th row: Purl.

5th row: Sl1. K1. psso. K6. *yo. K1. K2tog. K4. Rep from * to last 4 sts. K2. K2tog.

6th row: Purl.

7th row: Sl1. K1. psso. K6. *yo. K2tog. K5. Rep from * to last 2 sts. K2tog.

8th row: Purl to last 2 sts. P2togtbl. 42 {**49**-49-**56**} sts. Dec 1 st at V-neck edge only on next and every alt row 5 {**11**-5-**11**} times, then every 4th row from previous dec 10 {**8**-12-**10**} times. 26 {**29**-31-**34**} sts. Cont even in pat until armhole measures same length as Back to beg of shoulder shaping, ending on a 10th {**12th**-14th-**18th**} row of pat.

Shoulder shaping: Bind off 13 {**14**-15-**17**} sts beg next row. Purl 1 row. Bind off rem 13 {**15**-16-**17**} sts.

RIGHT FRONT

Work from ** to ** as given for Left Front.

Armhole and V-neck shaping: 1st row: (Right Side). Sl1. K1. psso. K1. *yo. K3. K2tog. K2. Rep from * to last st. K1.

2nd row: Bind off 3 sts. Purl to end of row.

3rd row: Sl1. K1. psso. K1. *yo. K2. K2tog. K3. Rep from * to last 4 sts. yo. (K2tog) twice.

4th row: Purl.

5th row: Sl1. K1. psso. K1. *yo. K1. K2tog. K4. Rep from * to last 2 sts. K2tog.

6th row: Purl.

7th row: Sl1. K1. psso. K1. *yo. K2tog. K5. Rep from * to last 7 sts. yo. K2tog. K3. K2tog.

8th row: P2tog. Purl to end of row. 42 {**49**-49-**56**} sts.
Proceed as follows to cont shaping V-neck only:

1st row: (Right Side). Sl1. K1. psso. K4. *Sl1. K1. psso. K5. yo. Rep from * to last st. K1.

2nd and alt rows: Purl.

3rd row: Sl1. K1. psso. K3. *Sl1. K1. psso. K4. yo. K1. Rep from * to last st. K1.

5th row: Sl1. K1. psso. K2. *Sl1. K1. psso. K3. yo. K2. Rep from * to last st. K1.

7th row: Sl1. K1. psso. K1. *Sl1. K1. psso. K2. yo. K3. Rep from * to last st. K1.

9th row: Sl1. K1. psso. *Sl1. K1. psso. K1. yo. K4. Rep from * to last st. K1.

11th row: Sl1. K2tog. psso. yo. K5. *Sl1. K1. psso. yo. K5. Rep from * to last st. K1. 36 {**43**-43-**50**} sts.

Sizes M and XL only: Dec 1 st at neck edge only, as established above, on next and every following alt row 4 times.

All Sizes: Dec 1 st at neck edge only, as established above, on every 4th row from previous dec 10 {**8**-12-**10**} times. 26 {**29**-31-**34**} sts.

Cont even in pat until armhole measures same length as Back to beg of shoulder shaping, ending on an 11th {**13th**-15th-**19th**} row.

Shoulder shaping: Bind off 13 {**14**-15-**17**} sts beg next row. Work 1 row even. Bind off rem 13 {**15**-16-**17**} sts.

SLEEVES

With smaller needles, cast on 57 sts.
Work 12 rows in Eyelet Rib Pat as given for Back, inc 3 sts evenly across last row. 60 sts.
Change to larger needles and proceed in Lace Pat as given for Back, inc 1 st at each end of needle on 5th and every following 6th {**6th**-4th-**4th**} row to 78 {**84**-90-**94**} sts, taking inc sts into stocking st.
Cont even in pat until work from beg measures 11½", ending with right side facing for next row.

Top Shaping: Bind off 2 sts beg next 2 rows. Dec 1 st each end of needle on next and every following alt row 12 times. Dec 1 st each end of needle on

following 6 rows. Bind off 3 sts beg next 4 rows. Bind off rem 24 {**30**-36-**40**} sts.

FINISHING

Pin garment pieces to measurements. Cover with a damp cloth leaving to dry.

Buttonhole and button band: Sew shoulder seams. With right side of work facing and circular needle, pick up and knit 63 sts up Right Front edge to V-neck shaping. Pick up and knit 42 {**44**-48-**50**} sts up Right Front V-neck edge to shoulder seam. K36 {**37**-40-**41**} from Back st holder, dec 2 sts evenly across. Pick up and knit 42 {**44**-48-**50**} sts down Left Front V-neck edge. Pick up and knit 63 sts down Left Front edge to lower edge. 244 {**249**-260-**265**} sts.

Next row: Knit.

Next row: K3. *Bind off 1 st. K9 (including st on needle after bind off). Rep from * 5 times more. Bind off 1 st. Knit to end of row.

Next row: Knit, casting on 2 sts over each bound off st to make a loop. Bind off purlwise (right side).

Sew in Sleeves. Sew side and sleeve seams. Sew buttons to correspond to button loops.

GIRL'S VERSION

BACK

With smaller needles, cast on 71 {**78**-85} sts.

1st row: (Right Side). P1. *P1. K2. yo. Sl1. K1. psso. P2. Rep from * to end of row.

2nd row: *K2. P4. K1. Rep from * to last st. K1.

3rd row: P1. *P1. K2tog. yo. K2. P2. Rep from * to end of row.

4th row: As 2nd row.

These 4 rows form Eyelet Rib Pat.
Work a further 2 {**4**-6} rows in Eyelet Rib Pat, inc 3 sts evenly across last row. 74 {**81**-88} sts.

Change to larger needles and proceed in Lace Pat as given for Back of Woman's Version (see page 74).
Cont in Lace Pat until work from beg measures approx 8¼ {**8½**-9}", ending on a 16th row of Lace Pat.

Armhole shaping: 1st row: (Right Side). Bind off 3 sts (1 st rem on needle after bind off). yo. K2. K2tog. K2. *yo. K3. K2tog. K2. Rep from * to last st. K1.

2nd row: Bind off 3 sts. Purl to end of row.

3rd row: Sl1. K1. psso. yo. K1. K2tog. K3. *yo. K2. K2tog. K3. Rep from * to last 4 sts. yo. K2. K2tog.

4th row: P2tog. Purl to end of row.

72

5th row: Sl1. K1. psso. K6. *yo. K1. K2tog. K4. Rep from * to last 2 sts. K2tog.
6th row: Purl.
7th row: Sl1. K1. psso. K6. *yo. K2tog. K5. Rep from * to last 7 sts. yo. K2tog. K3. K2tog.
8th row: P2tog. Purl to last 2 sts. P2togtbl. 60 {**67**-74} sts.

Beg with 1st row of Lace Pat, cont even in pat until armhole measures approx 5 {**5½**-6}", ending on a 10th {**16th**-22nd} row of Lace Pat.

Shoulder shaping: Bind off 8 {**9**-10} sts beg next 2 rows, then bind off 9 {**10**-11} sts beg following 2 rows. Leave rem 26 {**29**-32} sts on a st holder.

LEFT FRONT

With smaller needles, cast on 36 {36**-43} sts.
Work 6 {**8**-10} rows in Eyelet Rib Pat as given for Back inc 3 sts evenly across last row. 39 {**39**-46} sts.

Change to larger needles and proceed in Lace Pat as given for Back until work from beg measures approx 6¾ {**7**-7½}", ending on a 16th row of Lace Pat.**

Armhole and V-neck shaping: 1st row: (Right Side). Bind off 3 sts. yo. K2. K2tog. K2. *yo. K3. K2tog. K2. Rep from * to last 8 sts. yo. K3. K2tog. K1. K2tog.
2nd row: Purl.
3rd row: Sl1. K1. psso. yo. K1. K2tog. K3. *yo. K2. K2tog. K3. Rep from * to last 6 sts. yo. K2. (K2tog) twice.
4th row: Purl.
5th row: Sl1. K1. psso. K6. *yo. K1. K2tog. K4. Rep from * to last 4 sts. K2. K2tog.
6th row: Purl.
7th row: Sl1. K1. psso. K6. *yo. K2tog. K5. Rep from * to last 2 sts. K2tog.
8th row: Purl to last 2 sts. P2togtbl. 28 {**28**-35} sts. Dec 1 st at V-neck edge only on next and every alt row 4 times, then every 4th row from previous dec 6 {**4**-9} times. 17 {**19**-21} sts.

Cont even in pat until armhole measures same length as Back to beg of shoulder shaping, ending on a 10th {**16th**-22nd} row of Lace Pat.

Shoulder shaping: Bind off 8 {**9**-10} sts beg next row. Purl 1 row. Bind off rem 9 {**10**-11} sts.

RIGHT FRONT

Work from ** to ** as given for Left Front.

Armhole and V-neck shaping: 1st row: (Right Side). Sl1. K1. psso. K1. *yo. K3. K2tog. K2. Rep from * to last st. K1.
2nd row: Bind off 3 sts. Purl to end of row.
3rd row: Sl1. K1. psso. K1. *yo. K2. K2tog. K3. Rep from * to last 4 sts. yo. (K2tog) twice.
4th row: Purl.
5th row: Sl1. K1. psso. K1. *yo. K1. K2tog. K4. Rep from * to last 2 sts. K2tog.
6th row: Purl.
7th row: Sl1. K1. psso. K1. *yo. K2tog. K5. Rep from * to last 7 sts. yo. K2tog. K3. K2tog.
8th row: P2tog. Purl to end of row. 28 {**28**-35} sts.

Proceed as follows to cont shaping V-neck only:
1st row: (Right Side). Sl1. K1. psso. K4. *Sl1. K1. psso. K5. yo. Rep from * to last st. K1.
2nd and alt rows: Purl.
3rd row: Sl1. K1. psso. K3. *Sl1. K1. psso. K4. yo. K1. Rep from * to last st. K1.
5th row: Sl1. K1. psso. K2. *Sl1. K1. psso. K3. yo. K2. Rep from * last st. K1.
7th row: Sl1. K1. psso. K1. *Sl1. K1. psso. K2. yo. K3. Rep from * to last st. K1.
9th row: Sl1. K1. psso. *Sl1. K1. psso. K1. yo. K4. Rep from * to last st. K1.
Dec 1 st at V-neck edge only, as established above, on every 4th row from previous dec 6 {**4**-9} times more. 17 {**19**-21} sts.

Cont even in pat until armhole measures same length as Back to beg of shoulder shaping, ending on an 11th {**17th**-23rd} row of Lace Pat.

Shoulder shaping: Bind off 8 {**9**-10} sts beg next row. Work 1 row even. Bind off rem 9 {**10**-11} sts.

SLEEVES

With smaller needles, cast on 43 sts.
Work 6 {**8**-10} rows in Eyelet Rib Pat as given for Back, inc 3 sts evenly across last row. 46 sts.

Change to larger needles and proceed in Lace Pat as given for Back inc 1 st at each end of needle on next and every following 4th row to 58 {**64**-68} sts, taking inc sts into stocking st.

Cont even in pat until work from beg measures 6½", ending with right side facing for next row.

Top shaping: Bind off 2 st beg next 2 rows. Dec 1 st each end of needle on next and every following alt row 7 times. Bind off 3 sts beg next 4 rows. Bind off rem 26 {**32**-36} sts.

FINISHING
Pin garment pieces to measurements. Cover with a damp cloth leaving to dry.

Buttonhole and button band: Sew shoulder seams. With right side of work facing and circular needle, pick up and knit 35 {**37**-39} sts up Right Front edge to V-neck shaping. Pick up and knit 32 {**34**-38} sts up Right Front V-neck edge to shoulder seam. K26 {**29**-32} from Back st holder, dec 2 sts evenly across. Pick up and knit 32 {**34**-38} sts down Left Front V-neck edge. Pick up and knit 35 {**37**-39} sts down Left Front edge to lower edge. 158 {**171**-184} sts.
Next row: Knit.
Next row: K3. *Bind off 1 st. K6 {**7**-8} (including st on needle after bind off). Rep from * 3 times more. Bind off 1 st. Knit to end of row.
Next row: Knit, casting on 2 sts over each bound off st to make a loop. Bind off purlwise (right side).

Sew in sleeves. Sew side and sleeve seams. Sew buttons to correspond to button loops.

Lace Pattern

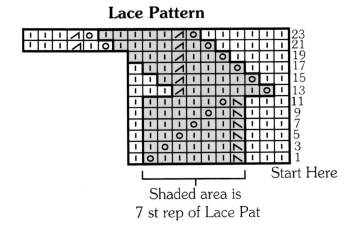

Shaded area is
7 st rep of Lace Pat

Key

☐ = Knit on Right Side, purl on Wrong Side

⊙ = yo

⟋ = K2tog

⟍ = Sl1. K1. psso.

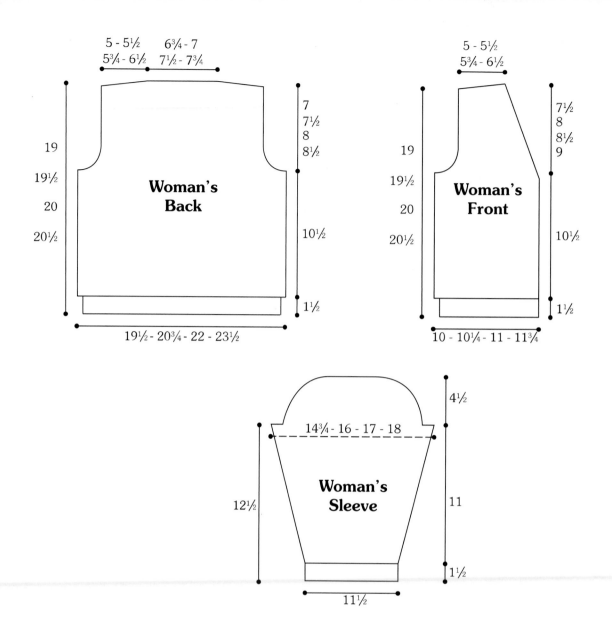

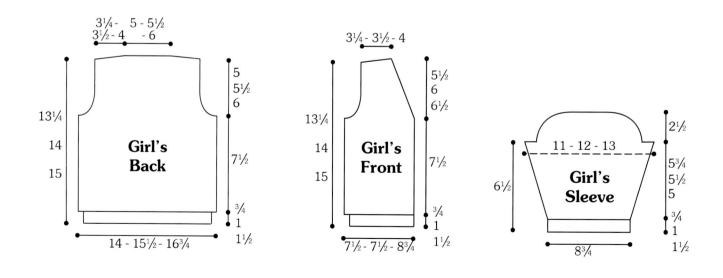

Woman's Back

5 - 5½
5¾ - 6½

6¾ - 7
7½ - 7¾

19

19½

20

20½

7
7½
8
8½

10½

1½

19½ - 20¾ - 22 - 23½

Woman's Front

5 - 5½
5¾ - 6½

19

19½

20

20½

7½
8
8½
9

10½

1½

10 - 10¼ - 11 - 11¾

Woman's Sleeve

14¾ - 16 - 17 - 18

4½

11

1½

12½

11½

Girl's Back

3¼ -   5 - 5½
3½ - 4   - 6

13¼

14

15

5
5½
6

7½

¾
1

1½

14 - 15½ - 16¾

Girl's Front

3¼ - 3½ - 4

13¼

14

15

5½
6
6½

7½

¾
1

1½

7½ - 7½ - 8¾

Girl's Sleeve

11 - 12 - 13

6½

2½

5¾
5½
5

¾
1

1½

8¾

13. Fur Look on the Bias Scarf   Easy

SIZE
Approx 6½" wide x 60" long.

MATERIALS
Bulky Weight Novelty Yarn: 1¾ oz (77 yds/50 g)

Variegated	**2**	**balls**

Sport Weight Yarn: 1¾ oz (133 yds/50 g)

Magenta	**1**	**ball**
Lilac	**1**	**ball**

Sample made with **Patons Astra** and **Patons Cha Cha.**

Size 7 (4.5 mm) knitting needles **or size needed for gauge.**

GAUGE SWATCH
18 sts and 30 rows = 4 ins in garter st with sport weight yarn.

STITCH GUIDE

M1 = make one st by picking up horizontal loop lying before next st and knitting into back of loop.

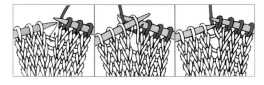

With Magenta, cast on 1 st.
1st row: (Right Side). (K1. P1. K1) all in st. 3 sts.
2nd and alt rows: Knit.
3rd row: (K1. M1) twice. K1. 5 sts.
5th row: K1. M1. Knit to last st. M1. K1.
6th row: Knit.
Last 2 rows form Inc Pat.
With Variegated, work 6 rows in Inc Pat. 13 sts.
With Lilac, work 6 rows in Inc Pat. 19 sts.
With Variegated, work 6 rows in Inc Pat. 25 sts.
With Magenta, work 6 rows in Inc Pat. 31 sts.

With Variegated, proceed as follows:
1st row: (Right Side). K1. M1. Knit to last 2 sts. K2tog. 31 sts.
2nd row: Knit.
Last 2 rows form Straight Pat.

With Variegated, work a further 4 rows in Straight Pat.
With Lilac, work 6 rows in Straight Pat.
With Variegated, work 6 rows in Straight Pat.
With Magenta, work 6 rows in Straight Pat.
Last 24 rows form Body Pat.
Cont in Body Pat until work from beg (measured along straight edge) measures approx 60", ending on a 6th row of Body Pat.

With Lilac, proceed as follows:
1st row: (Right Side). Sl1. K1. psso. Knit to last 2 sts. K2tog.
2nd row: Knit.
Last 2 rows form Dec Pat.
With Lilac, work a further 4 rows in Dec Pat. 25 sts.
With Variegated, work 6 rows in Dec Pat. 19 sts.
With Magenta, work 6 rows in Dec Pat. 13 sts.
With Variegated, work 6 rows in Dec Pat. 7 sts.
With Magenta, work 4 rows in Dec Pat. 3 sts.
Next row: (Right Side). Sl1. K2tog. psso. Fasten off.

14. Pullover with Star

Intermediate

SIZES

Chest measurement

4	23"
6	25"
8	26½"
10	28"

Finished Chest

4	30"
6	32½"
8	34½"
10	39"

Size Note: The instructions are written for size 4, with sizes 6, 8 and 10 in braces { }. Instructions will be easier to read if you circle all the numbers pertaining to your size. If only one number is given, it applies to all sizes.

MATERIALS

Chunky Weight Yarn: 3½ oz (148 yds/100g)

Sizes	4	6	8	10	
Grey	4	4	5	5	balls
Red	1	1	1	1	ball
Black	1	1	1	1	ball

Sample made with **Patons Shetland Chunky.**

Sizes 7 (4.5 mm) and 10 (6 mm) knitting needles **or size needed for gauge.** Pair of size 6 (4 mm) double-pointed knitting needles. Zipper 7" long.

GAUGE SWATCH

15 sts and 20 rows = 4" with larger needles in stocking st.

STITCH GUIDE

SL1P = Slip next st purlwise, keeping yarn at wrong side of work.

Note: When working from Chart X, carry yarn not in use loosely across **wrong side** of work but never over more than 3 sts. When it must pass over more than 3 sts, weave it over and under color in use on next st or at center point of sts it passes over. The colors are never twisted around one another.

When working from Chart XI, wind small balls of the colors to be used, one for each separate area of color in the design. Start new colors at appropriate points. To change colors, twist the two colors around each other where they meet, on **wrong side**, to avoid a hole.

BACK

With Grey and smaller needles cast on 57 {61**-**65**-**73**} sts.
****1st row: (Wrong Side).** Knit.
2nd and 3rd rows: With Black, knit.
4th and 5th rows: With Grey, K4. *Sl1P. K3. Rep from * to last 5 sts. Sl1P. K4.
6th and 7th rows: With Black, knit.
8th and 9th rows: With Grey, knit.***

Change to larger needles and proceed as follows:
1st and 2nd rows: With Black, knit (noting that 1st row is right side).
3rd row: With Red, K1 {**0**-2-**0**}. Work 1st row of Chart X in stocking st reading row from **right** to left, noting the 6 st rep will be worked 9 {**10**-10-**12**} times. With Red, K2 {**1**-3-**1**}.

4th row: With Red, P2 {**1**-**3**-**1**}. Work 2nd row of Chart X reading row from **left** to right. With Red, P1 {**0**-**2**-**0**}.
Chart X is now in position. *Chart X is shown on page 78.* Cont working Chart X to end of chart, thus ending with right side facing for next row.

With Black, knit 2 rows.
Next row: With Grey, knit.**

With Grey, cont work in stocking st until Back from beg measures 16 {**17½**-**19¼**-**20½**}", ending with right side facing for next row. Bind off.

Place markers 4¼ {**4¾**-**5¼**-**6½**}" in from each side along bound off edge to mark shoulders.

FRONT
Work from ** to ** as given for Back.

With Grey, cont in stocking st until work from beg measures 4 {**5**-**6**-**7**}", ending with right side facing for next row.

Next row: With Grey, K16 {**18**-**20**-**24**}. Work 1st row of Chart XI in stocking st across next 25 sts reading row from **right** to left. With Grey, K16 {**18**-**20**-**24**}.
Next row: With Grey, P16 {**18**-**20**-**24**}. Work 2nd row of Chart XI in stocking st across next 25 sts reading row from **left** to right. With Grey, P16 {**18**-**20**-**24**}.
Chart XI is now in position. *Chart XI is shown on page 78.* Cont working Chart XI to end of chart.

With Grey, cont in stocking st until Front from beg measures 9½ {**10¾**-**12**-**13**}", ending with right side facing for next row.

Zipper opening: Next row: K28 {**30**-**32**-**36**}. **Turn.** Leave rem sts on spare needle.
Cont in stocking st until Left Front measures 13½ {**14¾**-**16**-**17**}", ending with **wrong side** facing for next row.

Neck shaping: Next row: Bind off 7 sts (neck edge). Purl to end of row. 21 {**23**-**25**-**29**} sts.

Dec 1 st at neck edge on next 2 rows and following alt rows 3 times. 16 {**18**-**20**-**24**} sts. Cont even until

work from beg measures same length as Back, ending with right side facing for next row. Bind off.

With right side of work facing slip center st onto a safety pin. Join Grey to rem 28 {**30**-**32**-**36**} sts and knit to end of row.

Cont in stocking st until Right Front measures 13½ {**14¾**-**16**-**17**}", ending with right side facing for next row.

Neck shaping: Next row: Bind off 7 sts (neck edge). Knit to end of row. 21 {**23**-**25**-**29**} sts .

Dec 1 st at neck edge on next 2 rows and following alt rows 3 times. 16 {**18**-**20**-**24**} sts. Cont even until work from beg measures same length as Back, ending with **wrong side** facing for next row. Bind off.

SLEEVES
With Grey and smaller needles cast on 29 {**33**-**33**-**37**} sts. Work from *** to *** as given for Back, ending with right side facing for next row and inc 4 {**4**-**8**-**6**} sts evenly across last row. 33 {**37**-**41**-**43**} sts.

Change to larger needles and proceed as follows:
1st and 2nd rows: With Black, knit.
3rd row: With Red, K1 {**0**-**2**-**0**}. Work 1st row of Chart X, reading row from **right** to left, noting the 6 st rep will be worked 5 {**6**-**6**-**7**} times. With Red, K2 {**1**-**3**-**1**}.
4th row: With Red, P2 {**1**-**3**-**1**}. Work 2nd row of Chart X reading row from **left** to right. With Red, P1 {**0**-**2**-**0**}.
Chart X is now in position.
Cont working Chart X to end of chart inc 1 st each end of needle on 5th row. 35 {**39**-**43**-**45**} sts.

Next 2 rows: With Black, knit.
Next row: With Grey, knit, inc 1 st each end of needle. 37 {**41**-**45**-**47**} sts.
Cont in stocking st, inc 1 st each end of needle on every following 2nd {**2nd**-**4th**-**4th**} row to 41 {**45**-**49**-**51**} sts, then every following 4th {**4th**-**6th**-**6th**} row to 53 {**57**-**61**-**65**} sts.

Cont even in stocking st until sleeve from beg measures 10½ {**12**-**13½**-**15**}", ending with right side facing for next row. Bind off.

HOOD

With Grey and larger needles, cast on 73 {**77**-81-**85**} sts loosely.
Work 8 rows stocking st, ending with right side facing for next row.

9th and 10th rows: With Black, knit.
11th and 12th rows: With Grey, K4. *Sl1P. K3. Rep from * to last 5 sts. Sl1P. K4.
13th and 14th rows: With Black, knit.
15th and 16th rows: With Grey, knit.

Change to larger needles and proceed as follows:
1st row: With Black, knit.
2nd row: With Black, knit, inc 0 {**2**-4-**0**} sts evenly across. 73 {**79**-85-**85**} sts.
3rd row: Work 1st row of Chart X reading row from **right** to left, noting the 6 st rep will be worked 12 {**13**-14-**14**} times. With Red, K1.
4th row: With Red, P1. Work 2nd row of Chart X to end of row, reading row from **left** to right. Chart X is now in position.
Cont working Chart X to end of chart, ending with right side facing for next row.

With Black, knit 2 rows.
Next row: With Grey, knit.

With Grey, cont in stocking st until work from beg measures 8¼ {**8½**-8¾-**9**}", ending with right side facing for next row.

Hood shaping: Next row: K63 {**69**-75-**75**}. **Turn.**
Leave rem sts on a spare needle.
Next row: P53 {**59**-65-**65**}. **Turn.**
Next row: K43 {**49**-55-**55**}. **Turn.**
Next row: P33 {**39**-45-**45**}. **Turn.**
Next row: K23 {**29**-35-**35**}. **Turn.**
Next row: P13 {**19**-25-**25**}. Leave rem sts on st holder (center back). Break yarn leaving a long end.

FINISHING

Pin garment pieces to measurements. Cover with a damp cloth leaving to dry.

Zipper Edging: With right side of work facing, Grey and smaller needles, pick up and knit 14 sts down Left Front zipper opening, K1 from safety pin. Pick up and knit 14 sts up Right Front zipper opening. 29 sts. Bind off knitwise (**wrong side**).

Sew zipper in position under zipper edging. Sew shoulder seams.

Fold hood in half. Divide rem sts onto two needles and graft center back seam (see Diagram).
Fold cast on edge to inside of hood to form casing and sew in position leaving open at ends.
Sew hood to neck edge.

Cord: With Red and 2 double-pointed needles cast on 3 sts.
K3. *Slide sts to other end of needle without turning work. K3. Rep from * until cord measures 36". Bind off. Thread cord through hood casing opening. Tie a knot at each end of cord.
Place markers on Front and Back side edges 7 {**7¾**-8¼-**8¾**}" down from shoulder seams. Sew in sleeves between markers. Sew side and sleeve seams.

Grafting

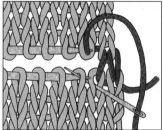 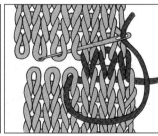

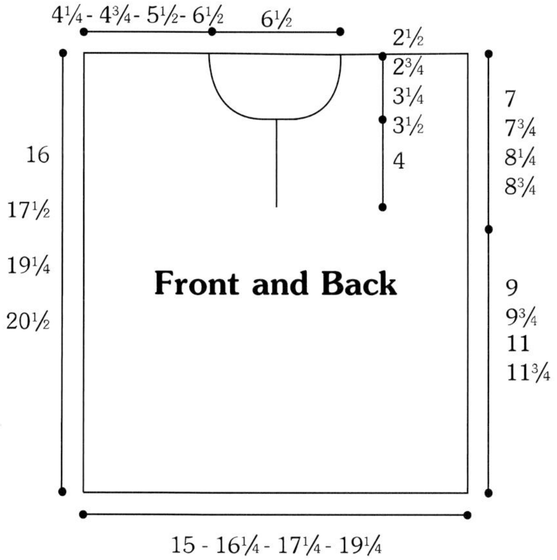
4¼ - 4¾ - 5½ - 6½
6½
2½
2¾
3¼
3½
4
16
17½
19¼
20½
7
7¾
8¼
8¾
9
9¾
11
11¾
Front and Back
15 - 16¼ - 17¼ - 19¼

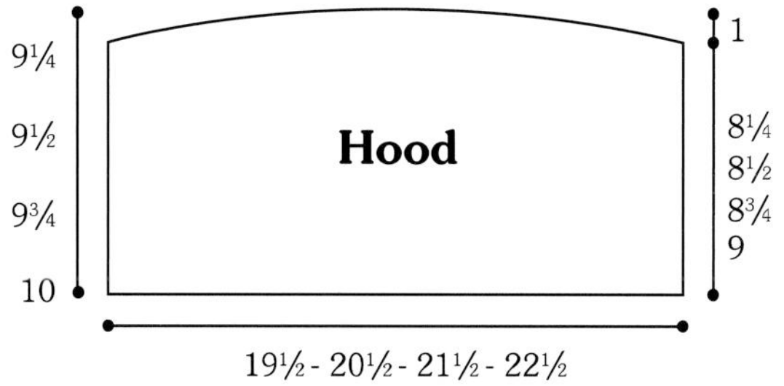
9¼
9½
9¾
10
Hood
1
8¼
8½
8¾
9
19½ - 20½ - 21½ - 22½

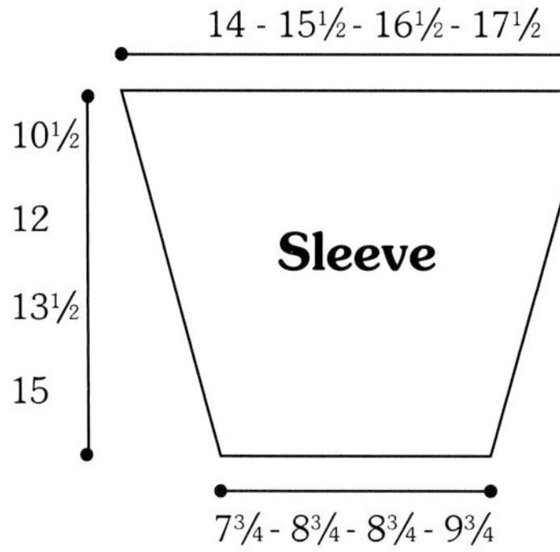
14 - 15½ - 16½ - 17½
10½
12
13½
15
Sleeve
7¾ - 8¾ - 8¾ - 9¾

Chart X

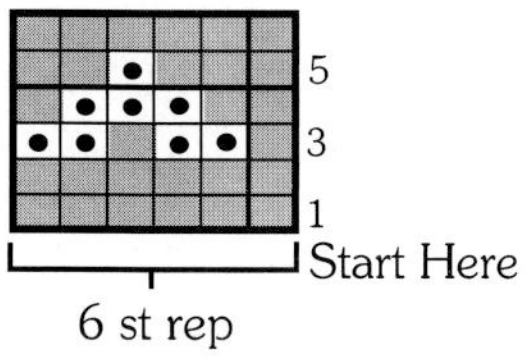
5
3
1
Start Here
6 st rep

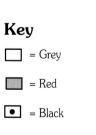

Key

☐ = Grey

▩ = Red

⊡ = Black

Chart XI

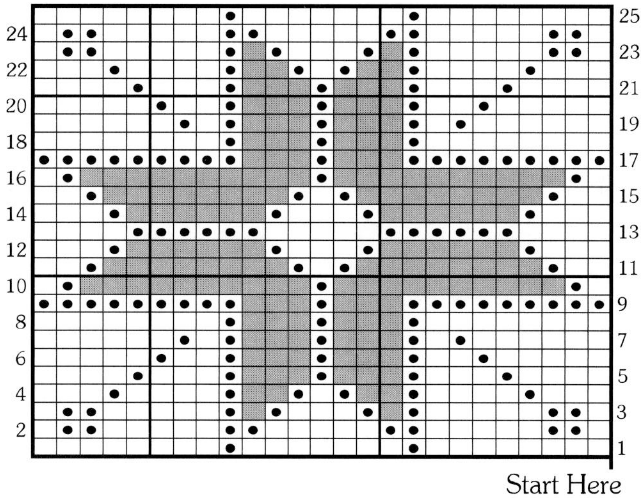
25
24
23
22
21
20
19
18
17
16
15
14
13
12
11
10
9
8
7
6
5
4
3
2
1
Start Here

15. Checkers Vest or Jacket

Intermediate

SIZES

Chest measurement

4	23"
6	25"
8	26½"
10	28"

Finished chest

4	31"
6	33"
8	35"
10	38"

Size Note: *Instructions are written for size 4, with sizes 6, 8 and 10 in braces { }. Instructions will be easier to read if you circle all the numbers pertaining to your size. If only one number is given, it applies to all sizes.*

MATERIALS

Chunky Weight Yarn: 3½ oz (160 yds/100 g)

Sizes	4	6	8	10	
Jacket					
Blue	3	3	4	4	balls
Ragg Mix	1	1	1	2	ball(s)
Cream	1	1	1	2	ball(s)
Vest					
Grey	2	2	3	3	balls
Ragg Mix	1	1	1	2	ball(s)
Cream	1	1	1	2	ball(s)

Samples made with **Patons Shetland Chunky.**

Sizes 7 (4.5 mm) and 10 (6 mm) knitting needles **or size needed for gauge.** One separating zipper. One st holder.

GAUGE SWATCH

15 sts and 20 rows = 4" with larger needles in stocking st.

JACKET

Note: When working from chart, wind small balls of the colors to be used, one for each separate area of color in the design. Start new colors at appropriate points. To change colors, twist the two yarns around each other where they meet on **wrong side** to avoid a hole.

BACK

With Blue and smaller needles, cast on 58 {**62**-66-**70**} sts.

1st row: (Right Side). K2. *P2. K2. Rep from * to end of row.

2nd row: P2. *K2. P2. Rep from * to end of row. Rep these 2 rows of (K2. P2) ribbing for 2", ending on a 2nd row and inc 1 st in center of last row. 59 {**63**-67-**71**} sts.

Change to larger needles and work Chart XII in stocking st until row 36 {**40**-46-**50**} of chart is complete reading **knit** rows from **right** to left and **purl** rows from **left** to right. *Chart XII is shown on page 84.*

Armhole shaping: Keeping cont of chart, bind off 3 {**4**-4-**4**} sts beg next 2 rows.

Dec 1 st each end of needle on next and following alt rows 2 {**2**-3-**3**} times. 47 {**49**-51-**55**} sts.

Cont working Chart XII until row 72 {**78**-86-**92**} of chart is complete.

Shoulder shaping: Bind off 6 sts beg next 4 rows. Leave rem 23 {**25**-27-**31**} sts on a st holder.

LEFT FRONT
With Blue and smaller needles, cast on 26 {30**-30-**34**} sts.
Work 2" in (K2. P2) ribbing as given for Back, ending on a 2nd row and inc 3 {**1**-3-**1**} st(s) evenly across last row. 29 {**31**-33-**35**} sts.**

Change to larger needles and work Chart XII in stocking st until row 36 {**40**-46-**50**} of chart is complete, reading **knit** rows from **right** to left and **purl** rows from **left** to right.

Armhole shaping: Keeping cont of chart, bind off 3 {**4**-4-**4**} sts beg next row.
Work 1 row even. Dec 1 st at armhole edge on next and following alt rows 2 {**2**-3-**3**} times. 23 {**24**-25-**27**} sts.

Cont working Chart XII until row 62 {**64**-74-**78**} of chart is complete.

Neck shaping: Next row: Work chart to last 6 {**6**-7-**8**} sts (neck edge). **Turn.** Leave rem sts on a safety pin.
Work 1 row even.
Dec 1 st at neck edge on next and every following alt row to 12 sts.
Cont working Chart XII until row 72 {**78**-86-**92**} of chart is complete.

Shoulder shaping: Bind off 6 sts beg next row. Work 1 row even. Bind off rem 6 sts.

RIGHT FRONT
Work from ** to ** as given for Left Front.

Change to larger needles and work Chart XII in stocking st until row 37 {**41**-47-**51**} of chart is complete, reading **knit** rows from **right** to left and **purl** rows from **left** to right.

Armhole shaping: Keeping cont of chart, bind off 3 {**4**-4-**4**} sts beg next row.
Dec 1 st at armhole edge on next and following alt rows 2 {**2**-3-**3**} times. 23 {**24**-25-**27**} sts.

Cont working Chart XII until row 62 {**64**-74-**78**} of chart is complete.

Neck shaping: Next row: Slip first 6 {**6**-7-**8**} sts onto a safety pin (neck edge). Rejoin yarn to next st and work chart to end of row.
Work 1 row even.
Dec 1 st at neck edge on next and every following alt row to 12 sts.
Cont working chart until row 73 {**79**-87-**93**} of chart is complete.

Shoulder shaping: Bind off 6 sts beg next row. Work 1 row even. Bind off rem 6 sts.

SLEEVES
With Blue and smaller needles, cast on 34 {**34**-38-**38**} sts.
Work 2" in (K2. P2) ribbing as given for Back, ending on a 2nd row and inc 3 {**5**-3-**5**} sts evenly across last row. 37 {**39**-41-**43**} sts.

Change to larger needles and proceed in stocking st inc 1 st each end of needle on 5th and every following 6th row to 51 {**53**-55-**59**} sts.

Cont even until Sleeve from beg measures 10½ {**12**-13½-**15**}", ending with right side facing for next row.

Shape top: Bind off 2 sts beg next 2 rows.
Dec 1 st each end of needle on next and every following alt rows to 31 {**31**-31-**35**} sts, then every row to 13 {**15**-15-**15**} sts. Bind off.

FINISHING
Pin garment pieces to measurements. Cover with a damp cloth leaving to dry.

Collar: Sew shoulder seams. With right side of work facing, smaller needles and Blue, K6 {**6**-7-**8**} from Right Front safety pin, pick up and knit 9 {**10**-14-**15**} sts up Right Front neck edge. K23 {**25**-27-**31**} from Back st holder, dec 3 sts evenly across. Pick up and knit 9 {**10**-14-**15**} sts down Left Front neck edge. K6 {**6**-7-**8**} from Left Front safety pin. 50 {**54**-66-**74**} sts.
Beg and ending on a 2nd row, work 2" in (K2. P2) ribbing as given for Back. Bind off loosely in ribbing.

Right Front Zipper Edging: With right side of work facing, smaller needles and Blue, pick up and knit 48 {**50**-56-**60**} sts up Right Front edge between cast on edge and bound off edge of Collar. Bind off knitwise (**wrong side**).

Left Front Zipper Edging: With right side of work facing, smaller needles and Blue, pick up and knit 48 {**50**-56-**60**} sts down Left Front edge between bound off edge of Collar and cast on edge. Bind off knitwise (**wrong side**).

Sew zipper in position under edgings.

VEST

Work Back, Left Front and Right Front as given for Jacket, substituting Grey for Blue.

FINISHING

Work Collar and Zipper Edgings as given for Jacket.

Armhole edging: With right side of work facing, smaller needles and Grey, pick up and knit 60 {**64**-72-**80**} sts evenly along armhole edge. Work 2 rows in garter st (knit every row). Bind off knitwise (**wrong side**).

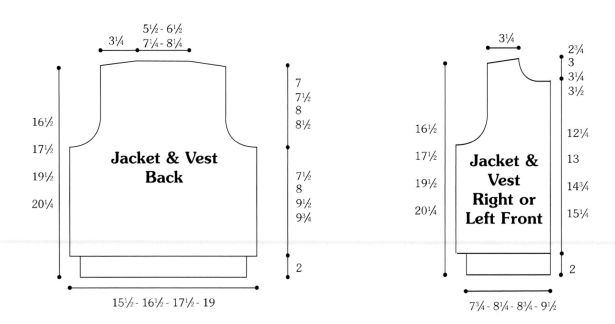

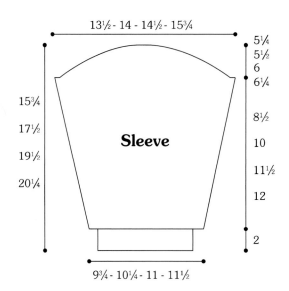

Chart XII

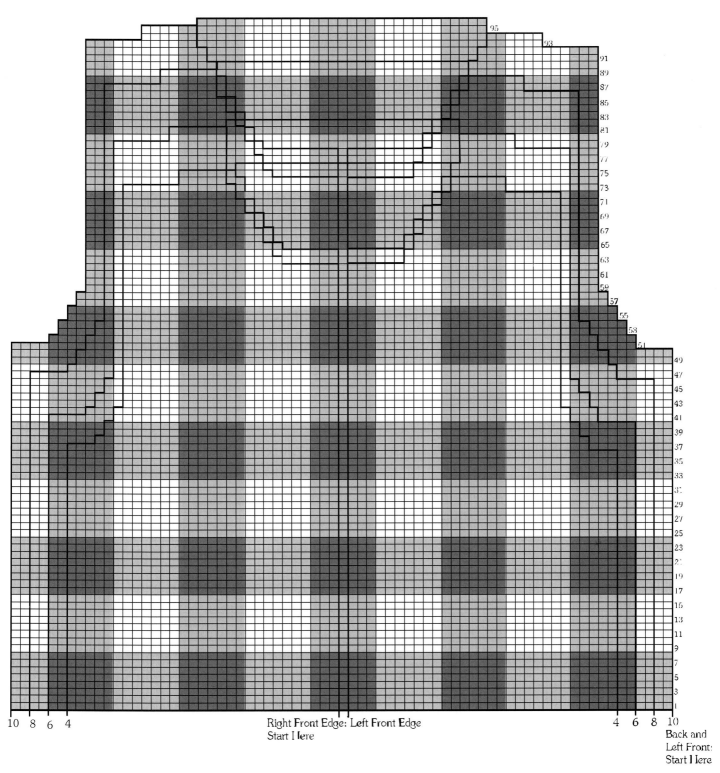

Right Front Edge: Left Front Edge
Start Here

Back and
Left Front:
Start Here

Key

■ = Blue or Grey

■ = Ragg Mix

□ = Cream

16. Hooded Sweatshirt

Easy

SIZES

Chest/Bust measurement

Petite	28"
Small	30-32"
Medium	34-36"
Large	38-40"

Finished bust

Petite	40"
Small	43"
Medium	46"
Large	49"

Size Note: The instructions are written for Petite with sizes Small, Medium and Large in braces { }. Instructions will be easier to read if you circle all the numbers pertaining to your size. If only one number is given, it applies to all sizes.

MATERIALS

Worsted Weight Yarn:
3½ oz (223 yds/100g)

Sizes	P	S	M	L	
Grey	**6**	**7**	**7**	**8**	balls
Dark Grey	**1**	**1**	**1**	**1**	ball
Light Grey	**1**	**1**	**1**	**1**	ball

Sample made with **Patons Classic Merino Wool.**

Sizes 7 (4.5 mm) and 10 (6 mm) knitting needles **or size needed for gauge.** Size 6 (4 mm) circular knitting needle 36" long. Two size 3 (3.25 mm) double-pointed needles. Zipper 8" long.

GAUGE SWATCH

20 sts and 26 rows = 4" with larger needles in stocking st.

FRONT

With Dark Grey and larger needles, cast on 101 {109**-115-**123**} sts.
1st row: (Right Side). With Grey, knit.
2nd row: P1. *K1. P1. Rep from * to end of row.
3rd row: K1. *P1. K1. Rep from * to end of row.
Rep last 2 rows (K1. P1) ribbing for 1½", ending with right side facing for next row.

Proceed in stocking st until Front from beg measures 15½ {**16**-16-**16½**}", ending with right side facing for next row.

Armhole shaping: Bind off 5 sts beg next 2 rows. Dec 1 st each end of needle on next 4 {**5**-5-**6**} rows. 83 {**89**-95-**101**} sts. Work 0 {**1**-1-**0**} row even. Cont in stocking st, working stripe pat as follows:
1st and 2nd rows: With Dark Grey.
3rd to 12th rows: With Light Grey.
13th and 14th rows: With Dark Grey.**

Change to Grey and work 2 {**2**-4-**6**} rows even.

Divide for front: Next row: K41 {**44**-47-**50**}. **Turn.** Leave rem sts on a spare needle.
Cont in stocking st until opening measures 3", ending with **wrong side** facing for next row.

Neck shaping: Next row: Bind off 6 sts. Purl to end of row.
Work 1 row even.

Bind off 3 sts beg next and following alt rows 3 times. 23 {**26**-29-**32**} sts. Dec 1 st at neck edge on next and following alt rows 3 times. 19 {**22**-25-**28**} sts. Work 3 rows even.

Shoulder shaping: Bind off 9 {**11**-12-**14**} sts beg next row.
Work 1 row even.
Bind off rem 10 {**11**-13-**14**} sts.
With right side of work facing, join Grey to rem 42 {**45**-48-**51**} sts. Bind off first st. Knit to end of row. Cont in stocking st until opening measures 3", ending with right side facing for next row.

Neck shaping: Next row: Bind off 6 sts. Knit to end of row.
Work 1 row even.
Bind off 3 sts beg next and following alt rows 3 times. 23 {**26**-29-**32**} sts.
Work 1 row even.
Dec 1 st at neck edge on next and following alt rows 3 times. 19 {**22**-25-**28**} sts.
Work 2 rows even.

Shoulder shaping: Bind off 9 {**11**-12-**14**} sts beg next row. Work 1 row even.
Bind off rem 10 {**11**-13-**14**} sts.

Back
Work from ** to ** as given for Front.

Change to Grey and cont in stocking st until Back measures same length as Front to beg of shoulder shaping, ending with right side facing for next row.

Shoulder shaping: Bind off 9 {**11**-12-**14**} sts beg next 2 rows. Bind off 10 {**11**-13-**14**} sts beg next 2 rows. Bind off rem 45 sts.

SLEEVES
With Dark Grey and larger needles, cast on 61 {**63**-65-**67**} sts.

1st row: (Right Side). With Grey, knit.
Proceed in (K1. P1) ribbing for 2" as given for Front, ending with right side facing for next row and inc 0 {**2**-2-**4**} sts evenly across last row. 61 {**65**-67-**71**} sts.

Proceed in stocking st, inc 1 st each end of needle on 5th and every following 6th row to 81 {**79**-91-**91**} sts, then every following 8th row to 87 {**91**-97-101} sts.

Cont even in stocking st until Sleeve from beg measures 16½ {**17½**-18-**19**}", ending with right side facing for next row.

Shape top: Bind off 5 sts beg next 2 rows.
Dec 1 st each end of next 4 {**4**-6-**6**} rows. 69 {**73**-75-**79**} sts. Bind off.

HOOD
Left half: With Grey and larger needles, cast on 50 sts.

Proceed in stocking st for 8", ending with right side facing for next row.

Dec 1 st beg next and every following alt row 12 times. 37 sts.
Work 1 row even.
Bind off 6 sts beg next and every following alt row 4 times.
Work 1 row even. Bind off rem 7 sts.

Right half: With Grey and larger needles, cast on 50 sts.

Proceed in stocking st for 8", ending with **wrong side** facing for next row.
Dec 1 st beg next and every following alt row 12 times. 37 sts.
Work 1 row even.
Bind off 6 sts beg next and every following alt row 4 times.
Work 1 row even. Bind off rem 7 sts.

FINISHING
Pin garment pieces to measurements, cover with a damp cloth and allow to dry.

Zipper Edging: With right side of work facing, Grey and larger needles, pick up and knit 14 sts down Left Front zipper opening and 14 sts up Right Front zipper opening. 28 sts.
Bind off knitwise (**wrong side**).

Sew zipper in position under edging.

Sew shoulder seams. Sew hood tog along back and top seams. Sew hood into neck opening.

Hood Casing: With right side of work facing, Grey and circular needle, pick up and knit 130 sts evenly around hood opening. **Do not** join. Working back and forth across needle, proceed as follows:
Beg with a purl row, work in stocking st for 3 rows. Bind off. Fold to inside of Hood to form casing and sew in position leaving open at ends.

Cord: With Dark Grey and 2 double-pointed needles cast on 3 sts. Work cord as follows: K3. *Slide sts to other end of needle without turning work. K3. Rep from * until cord measures 54". Bind off. Thread cord through hood casing. Tie a knot at each end of cord.

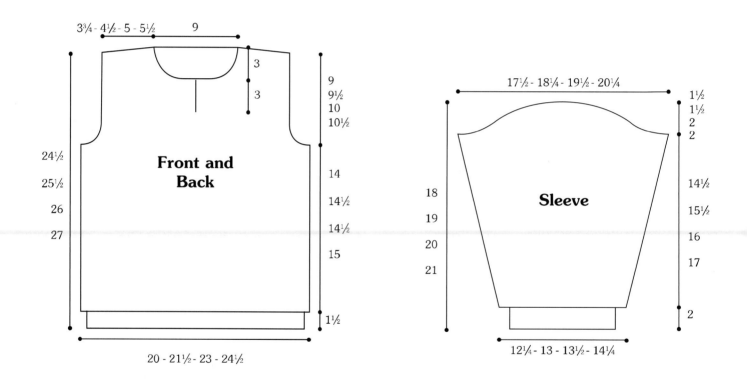

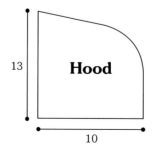

17. Festive Vest

Easy

SIZES

To fit chest measurement

2	21"
4	23"
6	25"

Finished chest measurement

2	25"
4	27"
6	29"

Size Note: Instructions are written for size 2 yrs, with sizes 4 and 6 yrs in braces { }. Instructions will be easier to read if you circle all the numbers pertaining to your size. If only one number is given, it applies to all sizes.

MATERIALS

Bulky Weight Novelty Yarn: 1¾ oz (77 yds/50 g)

Sizes	2	4	6	
Lime/Purple Variegated	**2**	**2**	**3**	**balls**

Sample made with **Patons Cha Cha.**

Size 11 (8 mm) knitting needles **or size needed for gauge.**

GAUGE SWATCH

11 sts and 16 rows = 4" in stocking st.

Note: Vest is knitted in one piece.

Cast on 62 {**67**-72} sts loosely.
Work 5 rows garter st (knit every row), inc 6 {**7**-8} sts evenly across last row. 68 {**74**-80} sts.
Next row: (Right Side). Knit.
Next row: K3. Purl to last 3 sts. K3.
Rep last 2 rows until work from beg measures 4 {**4½**-5}", ending with right side facing for next row.

Divide for armholes: Next row: K15 {**16**-18}. Bind off 4 sts. K30 {**34**-36} (including st on needle after bind off). Bind off 4 sts. K15 {**16**-18}. Cont on last 15 {**16**-18} sts for Left Front. Leave rem sts on a spare needle.

LEFT FRONT

1st row: (Wrong Side). K3. Purl to last 3 sts. K3.
2nd row: Knit to last 5 sts. K2tog. K3.
3rd row: As 1st row.
4th row: Knit.
Rep last 4 rows 4 {**3**-5} times more. 10 {**12**-12} sts.
Cont even, having 3 garter sts at V-neck and armhole edges, until armhole measures 5 {**5½**-6}", ending with right side facing for next row. Bind off.

Back: With **wrong side** of work facing, rejoin yarn to 30 {**34**-36} sts for Back.
Next row: (Wrong Side). K3. Purl to last 3 sts. K3.
Next row: Knit.
Rep last 2 rows until armhole measures 5 {**5½**-6}", ending with right side facing for next row. Bind off. Place markers 10 {**12**-12} sts in from side edges for shoulders.

88

Right Front: With **wrong side** of work facing, rejoin yarn to 15 {**16**-18} sts for Right Front.

1st row: (**Wrong Side**). K3. Purl to last 3 sts. K3.

2nd row: K3. K2tog. Knit to end of row.

3rd row: As 1st row.

4th row: Knit.

Rep last 4 rows 4 {**3**-5} times more. 10 {**12**-12} sts. Cont even, having 3 garter sts at V-neck and armhole edges, until armhole measures 5 {**5½**-6}", ending with right side facing for next row. Bind off.

FINISHING

Sew shoulder seams.

Ties: (make 2). Cast on 30 sts. Bind off.
Sew ties to beg of front edges at V-neck shaping as shown in picture.

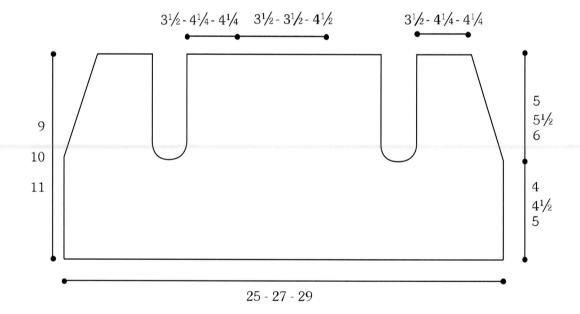

21

SCIENCE
An Introductory Study
9

18. Party Girl Collar and Skirt

Easy

SIZES

Collar
One size to fit child 2-6 yrs.

Skirt
To fit 2 (**4**-6) yrs.

Size Note: *Instructions are written for size 2 yrs, with sizes 4 and 6 yrs in braces { }. Instructions will be easier to read if you circle all the numbers pertaining to your size. If only one number is given, it applies to all sizes.*

MATERIALS

Bulky Weight Novelty Yarn: 1¾ oz (77 yds/50 g)
Collar

Red/Purple Variegated		**1**	**ball**

Skirt

Sizes	**2**	**4**	**6**	
Red/Purple Variegated	**2**	**2**	**3**	**balls**

Samples made with **Patons Cha Cha.**

Size 11 (8 mm) knitting needles for Collar. Size 10½ (6.5 mm) circular knitting needle 16" long for Skirt **or size needed for gauge.** ¾ yard of ¾" wide elastic for Skirt.

GAUGE SWATCH

Skirt: 13 sts and 19 rows = 4" with size 10½ needles in stocking st.
Collar: 11 sts and 16 rows = 4" with size 11 needles in stocking st.

COLLAR

With size 11 needles, cast on 16 sts.
Proceed in stocking st until work from beg measures 10", ending with right side facing for next row. Bind off.

To gather ends, thread yarn through cast on and bound off edges and tighten. Fasten securely.

Ties: (make 2). Cast on 30 sts. Bind off. Sew in position at ends of Collar.

SKIRT

With size 10½ circular needle, cast on 73 {**75**-79} sts. Join in rnd. Place marker on first st.
Knit in rnds until work from beg measures 9 {**10½**-11½}". Bind off.

Cut elastic to waist measurement and sew ends of elastic tog. Work herringbone st over elastic on wrong side at waist.

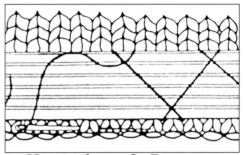

Herringbone St Diagram

19. Tulip Lace Dress with Blanket — Intermediate

Sizes

Dress

Chest measurement

6 mos	17"
12 mos	19"
18 mos	21"
2 yrs	21½"
3 yrs	22½"

Finished chest

6 mos	18"
12 mos	20½"
18 mos	22¼"
2 yrs	23½"
3 yrs	25"

Size Note: Instructions are written for size 6 mos, with sizes 12 mos, 18 mos, 2 yrs, and 3 yrs in braces { }. Instructions will be easier to read if you circle all the numbers pertaining to your size. If only one number is given, it applies to all sizes.

Blanket: Finished measurements: Approx 39¼" x 42".

MATERIALS

Sport Weight Yarn: 1¾ oz (136 yds/50 g)

Dress

Sizes	6 mos	12 mos	18 mos	2 yrs	3 yrs	
White	4	4	4	5	5	balls
Pale Pink	1	1	2	2	2	ball(s)
Aqua	1	1	1	1	1	ball

Blanket

White	10	balls
Pale Pink	6	balls
Aqua	1	ball

Samples made with **Patons Grace.**

Sizes 3 (3¼ mm) and 5 (3¾ mm) knitting needles. Sizes 3 (3¼ mm) and 7 (4½ mm) circular knitting needles 36" long, **or sizes needed for gauge.** 2 buttons and 4 small metal snap fasteners for Dress.

GAUGE

23 sts and 31 rows = 4" in stocking st with US 5 needles.
22 sts and 30 rows = 4" in stocking st with US 7 needles.

STITCH GUIDE

MB = [(K1. yo) 3 times. K1] all in next st. Slip 6th, 5th, 4th, 3rd, 2nd and first sts separately over 7th st. One st rem. Bobble complete.

Dress

Note: When working from chart, carry colors not in use loosely across **wrong side** of work. The colors are never twisted around one another.

FRONT

With Pale Pink and larger needles, cast on 87 {87**-91-**91**-110} sts.
Beg with a knit row, work 4 rows stocking st.
Next row: (Right Side). (Fold line). K1 {**1**-1-**1**-2}. *K2tog. yo. Rep from * to last 2 sts. K2.
Beg with a purl row, work 5 rows stocking st.

Work Chart XIII in stocking st to end of chart, reading **knit** rows from **right** to left and **purl** rows from **left** to right, noting 4 st rep will be worked 21 {**21**-22-**22**-27} times. Break Pale Pink and Aqua. Chart XIII shown on page 99.

With White, work 4 rows stocking st.

Proceed in Tulip Lace Pat as follows:
1st row: (Right Side). K5. *K2tog. yo. K1. yo. Sl1. K1. psso.** K13 {**13**-14-**14**-14}. Rep from * to last 10 sts. Rep from * to ** once. K5.
2nd and alt rows: Purl.
3rd row: K4. *K2tog. yo. K3. yo. Sl1. K1. psso.** K11 {**11**-12-**12**-12}. Rep from * to last 11 sts. Rep from * to ** once. K4.
5th row: K3. *(K2tog. yo) twice. K1. (yo. Sl1. K1. psso) twice.** K9 {**9**-10-**10**-10}. Rep from * to last 12 sts. Rep from * to ** once. K3.
7th row: K2. *(K2tog. yo. K1) twice. (yo. Sl1. K1. psso. K1) twice.** K6 {**6**-7-**7**-7}. Rep from * to last 13 sts. Rep from * to ** once. K1.
9th row: K1. *K2tog. yo. K2. K2tog. yo. K1. yo. Sl1. K1. psso. K2. yo. Sl1. K1. psso.** K5 {**5**-6-**6**-6}. Rep from * to last 14 sts. Rep from * to ** once. K1.
11th row: K4. *K2tog. yo. K3. yo. Sl1. K1. psso.** K11 {**11**-12-**12**-12}. Rep from * to last 11 sts. Rep from * to ** once. K4.
13th row: K3. *K2tog. yo. K5. yo. Sl1. K1. psso. K9 {**9**-10-**10**-10}.** Rep from * to last 12 sts. Rep from * to ** once. K3.
15th row: K2. *K2tog. yo. K1. yo. Sl1. K1. psso. K1. K2tog. yo. K1. yo. Sl1. K1. psso.** K7 {**7**-8-**8**-8}. Rep from * to last 13 sts. Rep from * to ** once. K2.
17th row: K1. *K2tog. yo. K1. MB. K1. yo. Sl1. K2tog. psso. yo. K1. MB. K1. yo. Sl1. K1. psso.** K5 {**5**-6-**6**-6}. Rep from * to last 14 sts. Rep from * to ** once. K1.
19th row: K7. *MB. K17 {**17**-18-**18**-18}. Rep from * to last 8 sts. MB. K7.
20th row: Purl.
These 20 rows complete Tulip Lace Pat.

Proceed in eyelet pat as follows:
1st row: (Right Side). Knit.
2nd and alt rows: Purl.
3rd row: Knit.
5th row: K2 {**2**-4-**4**-4}. *K2tog. yo. K7. Rep from * to last 4 {**4**-6-**6**-7} sts. K2tog. yo. K2 {**2**-4-**4**-5}.
7th and 9th rows: Knit.
11th row: K6 {**6**-8-**8**-8}. *K2tog. yo. K7. Rep from * to last 0 {**0**-2-**2**-3} sts. K0 {**0**-2-**2**-3}.
12th row: Purl.
These 12 rows form eyelet pat.

Cont in eyelet pat shaping sides by dec 1 st each end of needle on next and following 2nd {**4th**-4th-**4th**-4th} rows until there are 51 {**69**-69-**79**-70} sts.
Sizes 12, 18 mos and 2 yrs only: Cont in eyelet pat, dec 1 st each end of needle on following alt rows until there are {**57**-63-**67**} sts.

All Sizes: Cont even in eyelet pat until work from fold line measures 10½ {**11½**-13-**14¼**-15½}", ending with right side facing for next row.

Shape armholes: Keeping cont of pat, bind off 2 {**3**-4-**4**-4} sts beg next 2 rows. 47 {**51**-55-**59**-62} sts. Dec 1 st each end of needle on next and every following alt row to 43 {**45**-49-**51**-54} sts.**
Work a further 9 rows in pat, thus ending with right side facing for next row.

Shape neck: Next row: Pat across 16 {**17**-19-**19**-20} sts (neck edge). **Turn.** Leave rem sts on a spare needle.
Work 1 row even in pat.
Keeping cont of pat, dec 1 st at neck edge on next and following alt rows until there are 11 {**12**-13-**13**-14} sts.
Work 7 {**9**-9-**9**-11} rows even in pat. Bind off.

With right side of work facing, slip next 11 {**11**-11-**13**-14} sts from spare needle onto a st holder. Join yarn to rem sts and pat to end of row.
Work to correspond to other side.

BACK

Work from ** to ** as given for Front.
Work a further 17 {**17**-19-**19**-19} rows in pat, thus ending with right side facing for next row.

Shape neck: Next row: Pat across 14 {**15**-17-**17**-18} sts (neck edge). **Turn.** Leave rem sts on a spare needle.

Work 1 row even in pat.

Keeping cont of pat, dec 1 st at neck edge on next and following alt rows until there are 11 {**12**-13-**13**-14} sts. Work 9 rows even in pat.

Shape strap: Cont in stocking st, dec 1 st each end of next row. 9 {**10**-11-**11**-12} sts. Place a marker at each end of last row.

Purl 1 row.

Next row: Sl1. K1. psso. K1 {**2**-2-**2**-3}. K2tog. yo. K2 {**2**-3-**3**-3}. K2tog (buttonhole made). 7 {**8**-9-**9**-10} sts.

Purl 1 row.

Dec 1 st each end of next row. 5 {**6**-7-**7**-8} sts.

Purl 1 row. Bind off.

With right side of work facing, slip next 15 {**15**-15-**17**-18} sts from spare needle onto a st holder. Join yarn to rem sts and pat to end of row.

Work to correspond to other side.

FINISHING

Back edging: With right side of work facing, Pale Pink and smaller circular needle, pick up and knit 34 {**38**-40-**42**-44} sts up Right Back armhole edge to marker on strap. Pick up and knit 14 {**15**-16-**16**-17} sts around end of Strap to opposite marker. Pick up and knit 11 {**11**-13-**13**-13} sts down Right Back neck edge. K15 {**15**-15-**17**-18} from Back st holder. Pick up and knit 11 {**11**-13-**13**-13} sts up Left Back neck edge to marker on left strap. Pick up and knit 14 {**15**-16-**16**-17} sts around end of Strap to opposite marker. Pick up and knit 34 {**38**-40-**42**-44} sts down Left Back armhole edge. 133 {**143**-153-**159**-166} sts.

Beg with a purl row, work 3 rows stocking st.

Next row: (Right Side). (Fold line). K1. *K2tog. yo. Rep from * to last 2 {**2**-2-**2**-1} st(s). K2 {**2**-2-**2**-1}.

Beg with a purl row, work 3 rows stocking st.

Bind off.

Front Neck edging: With right side of work facing, Pale Pink and smaller needles, pick up and knit 16 {**18**-20-**20**-22} sts down Left Front neck edge. K11 {**11**-11-**13**-14} from Front st holder. Pick up and knit 16 {**18**-20-**20**-22} sts up Right Front neck edge. 43 {**47**-51-**53**-58} sts.

Beg with a purl row, work 3 rows stocking st.

Next row: (Right Side). (Fold line). K1. *K2tog. yo. Rep from * to last 2 {**2**-2-**2**-1} st(s). K2 {**2**-2-**2**-1}

Beg with a purl row, work 3 rows stocking st.

Bind off.

Front Armhole edging: With right side of work facing, Pale Pink and smaller needles, pick up and knit 30 {**34**-36-**38**-40} sts up Left Front armhole from side seam to bind off edge.

Beg with a purl row, work 3 rows stocking st.

Next row: (Right Side). K1. *K2tog. yo. Rep from * to last st. K1. (fold line).

Beg with a purl row, work 3 rows stocking st.

Bind off.

Rep on Right Front armhole edge, beg at bound off edge and ending at side seam.

Sew side and armhole edging seams. Fold all edgings to **wrong side** along fold line and sew in position. Sew on buttons to correspond to buttonholes. Sew 1 set of snap fasteners on either side of button on Straps.

Blanket

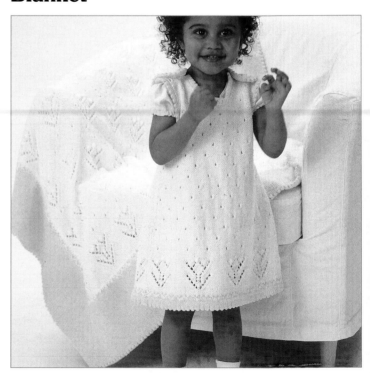

Center Section

With White and larger circular needle, cast on 148 sts. Beg with a knit row, work 2 rows stocking st.

***Proceed in Tulip Lace Pat for 20 rows as given for size 18 mos of Front of Dress.

Proceed in eyelet pat as follows:

1st row: (Right Side). Knit.

2nd and alt rows: Purl.
3rd row: Knit.
5th row: K9. *K2tog. yo. K7. Rep from * to last 4 sts. K4.
7th and 9th rows: Knit.
11th row: K4. *K2tog. yo. K7. Rep from * to end of row.
13th and 15th rows: Knit.
16th row: Purl.***
Rep from *** to *** 4 times more.

Work a further 20 rows in Tulip Lace Pat.
Beg with a knit row, work 2 rows stocking st.
Bind off.

Side Sections
With White and larger circular needle, pick up and knit 156 sts along side of Center Section.
Purl 1 row.
Work Chart XIII in stocking st to end of chart, reading **knit** rows from **right** to left and **purl** rows from **left** to right, noting side incs on 3rd row of chart. 158 sts.
Chart XIII shown on page 99.
With Pale Pink, cont in stocking st inc 1 st each end of next and following alt rows until there are 194 sts.
Purl 1 row.
Next row: (Right Side). K1. *K2tog. yo. Rep from * to last st. K1 (fold line).
Purl 1 row.
Dec 1 st each end of needle on next and following alt rows until there are 156 sts.
Purl 1 row. Bind off.
Rep on opposite side edge.

Top or Bottom Sections
With White and larger circular needle, pick up and knit 148 sts across top of Center Section.
Purl 1 row.
Work Chart XIV in stocking st to end of chart, reading **knit** rows from **right** to left and **purl** rows from **left** to right, noting side incs on 3rd row of chart. 150 sts.
With Pale Pink, cont in stocking st inc 1 st each end of next and following alt rows until there are 186 sts.
Purl 1 row.

Next row: (Right Side). (Fold line). K1. *K2tog. yo. Rep from * to last st. K1
Purl 1 row.
Dec 1 st each end of needle on next and following alt rows until there are 148 sts.
Purl 1 row. Bind off.
Rep on bottom of Center Section.

Sew 4 corner seams. Fold to **wrong side** along fold line and sew in position.

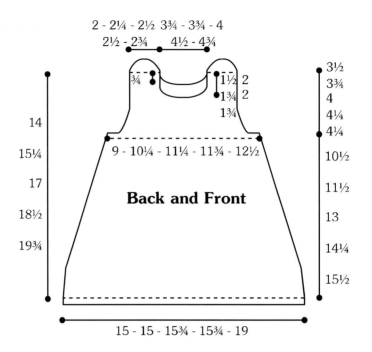

2 - 2¼ - 2½ 3¾ - 3¾ - 4

2½ - 2¾   4½ - 4¾

¾   1½ 2
                      1¾ 2
                      1¾

3½
3¾
4
4¼
4¼

14

15¼

17

18½

19¾

9 - 10¼ - 11¼ - 11¾ - 12½

10½

11½

13

14¼

15½

Back and Front

15 - 15 - 15¾ - 15¾ - 19

Chart XIII

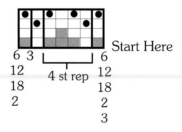

Start Here

6 3   6
12   12
18   18
2   2
                3

4 st rep

Chart XIV

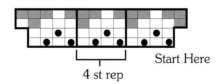

Start Here

4 st rep

Key

☐ = White

▨ = Pale Pink

⊡ = Aqua

99

20. Raglan Cables Set

Sizes

Chest measurement

6 mos	17"
12 mos	19"
18 mos	21"
2 yrs	21½"
3 yrs	22½"

Finished chest

6 mos	21"
12 mos	24½"
18 mos	26"
2 yrs	28"
3 yrs	30"

Size Note: Instructions are written for size 6 mos, with sizes 12 mos, 18 mos, 2 yrs, and 3 yrs in braces { }. Instructions will be easier to read if you circle all the numbers pertaining to your size. If only one number is given, it applies to all sizes.

MATERIALS

Sport Weight Yarn: 1¾ oz (136 yds/50 g)

Cardigan

Sizes	6 mos	12 mos	18 mos	2 yrs	3 yrs	
Blue	6	7	7	8	8	balls

Hat

Blue	2	balls

Samples made with **Patons Grace.**

Sizes 3 (3¼ mm) and 5 (3¾ mm) knitting needles **or size needed for gauge.** Cable needle. 3 st holders. 2 safety pins. 5 buttons.

GAUGE SWATCH

28 sts and 32 rows = 4" with larger needles in pat.

STITCH GUIDE

C6B = Slip next 3 sts onto a cable needle and leave at back of work. K3, then K3 from cable needle.

Panel Pat (worked over 6 sts)
1st row: (Right Side). K6.
2nd and alt rows: Purl.
3rd row: C6B.
5th and 7th rows: K6.
8th row: Purl.
These 8 rows form Panel Pat.

Cardigan

BACK

With smaller needles, cast on 69 {**81**-87-**93**-99} sts.

Sizes 6 mos, 12 mos and 2 yrs only: 1st row: (Right Side). *P3. K3. Rep from * to last 3 sts. P3.
2nd row: K1. *P1. K1. Rep from * to end of row. Rep last 2 rows 4 times more.

Change to larger needles and proceed in pat as follows:
Next row: (Right Side). (Increase row). P3. (K3. P3. K1. Inc 1 st in next st. K1. P3) 5 {**6**-7} times. K3. P3. 74 {**87**-**100**} sts.

Next row: (K1. P1) 3 times. *K2. P6. K2. P1. K1. P1. Rep from * to last 3 sts. K1. P1. K1.

Next row: P3. *K3. P2. Work 1st row of Panel Pat. P2. Rep from * to last 6 sts. K3. P3.

Next row: (K1. P1) 3 times. *K2. Work 2nd row of Panel Pat. K2. P1. K1. P1. Rep from * to last 3 sts. K1. P1. K1.

Panel Pat is now in position.

Sizes 18 mos and 3 yrs only: 1st row: (Right Side). *K3. P3. Rep from * to last 3 sts. K3.

2nd row: P1. *K1. P1. Rep from * to end of row. Rep last 2 rows 4 times more.

Change to larger needles and proceed in pat as follows:

Next row: (Right Side). (Increase row). K3. P3. (K3. P3. K1. Inc 1 st in next st. K1. P3) {6-7} times. K3. P3. K3. {93-106} sts.

Next row: (P1. K1) 4 times. P1. *K2. P6. K2. P1. K1. P1. Rep from * to last 6 sts. (K1. P1) 3 times.

Next row: K3. P3. *K3. P2. Work 1st row of Panel Pat. P2. Rep from * to last 9 sts. K3. P3. K3.

Next row: (P1. K1) 4 times. P1. *K2. Work 2nd row of Panel Pat. K2. P1. K1. P1. Rep from * to last 6 sts. (K1. P1) 3 times.

Panel Pat is now in position.

All Sizes: Cont even in pat until work from beg measures 6½ {7-7¾-8½-9¼}", ending with right side facing for next row.

Raglan shaping: Keeping cont of pat, bind off 5 {5-7-7-7} sts beg next 2 rows. 64 {77-79-86-92} sts.

Next row: (Right Side). P1. Sl1. K1. psso. Pat to last 3 sts. K2tog. P1.

Next row: K1. P1. Pat to last 2 sts. P1. K1. Rep last 2 rows 16 {14-16-16-16} times more. 30 {47-45-52-58} sts.

Next row: (Right Side). P1. Sl1. K1. psso. Pat to last 3 sts. K2tog. P1.

Next row: K1. P2tog. Pat to last 3 sts. P2togtbl. K1. Rep last 2 rows 0 {4-3-4-5} times more. Leave rem 26 {27-29-32-34} sts on a st holder.

RIGHT FRONT

With smaller needles, cast on 33 {42-45-45-48} sts.

Sizes 6 mos, 18 mos and 2 yrs only: 1st row: (Right Side). *K3. P3. Rep from * to last 3 sts. K3.

2nd row: *P1. K1. Rep from * to last st. P1. Rep last 2 rows 4 times more.

Change to larger needles and proceed in pat as follows:

1st row: (Right Side). (Increase row). (K3. P3. K1. Inc 1 st in next st. K1. P3) 2 {3-3} times. K3. P3. K3. 35 {48-48} sts.

2nd row: (P1. K1) 4 times. P1. *K2. P6. K2. P1. K1. P1. Rep from * to end of row.

3rd row: (K3. P2. Work 1st row of Panel Pat. P2) 2 {3-3} times. K3. P3. K3.

4th row: (P1. K1) 4 times. P1. *K2. Work 2nd row of Panel Pat. K2. P1. K1. P1. Rep from * to end of row. Panel Pat is now in position.

Sizes 12 mos and 3 yrs only: 1st row: (Right Side). *K3. P3. Rep from * to end of row.

2nd row: *K1. P1. Rep from * to end of row. Rep last 2 rows 4 times more.

Change to larger needles and proceed in pat as follows:

1st row: (Right Side). (Increase row). (K3. P3. K1. Inc 1 st in next st. K1. P3) {3-4} times. (K3. P3) {1-0} time(s). {45-52} sts.

2nd row: (K1. P1) {3-0} times. *K2. P6. K2. P1. K1. P1. Rep from * to end of row.

3rd row: (K3. P2. Work 1st row of Panel Pat. P2) {3-4} times. (K3. P3) {1-0} time(s).

4th row: (K1. P1) {3-0} times. *K2. Work 2nd row of Panel Pat. K2. P1. K1. P1. Rep from * to end of row. Panel Pat is now in position.

All Sizes: Cont even in pat until work from beg measures 6½ {7-7¾-8½-9¼}", ending with **wrong side** facing for next row.

Raglan shaping: Next row: Bind off 5 {5-7-7-7} sts. Pat to end of row. 30 {40-41-41-45} sts.

Next row: Pat to last 3 sts. K2tog. P1.

Next row: K1. P1. Pat to end of row. Rep last 2 rows 12 {13-13-14-15} times more. 17 {26-27-26-29} sts.

Neck shaping: With right side of work facing, slip first 6 {8-8-8-8} sts onto a safety pin. Rejoin yarn to rem 11 {18-19-18-21} sts and proceed as follows:

Next row: (Right Side). Sl1. K1. psso. Pat to last 3 sts. K2tog. P1.

Next row: Pat to last 2 sts. P2togtbl. Rep last 2 rows 0 {0-1-1-0} time(s) more. 8 {15-13-12-18} sts.

Size 6 mos only: Next row: (Right Side). Sl1. K1. psso. Pat 3 sts. K2tog. P1. 6 sts.
Next row: Work even in pat.
Next row: Sl1. K1. psso. K1. K2tog. P1. 4 sts.
Next row: P4.
Next row: Sl1. K1. psso. K2tog. 2 sts.
Next row: P2.
Next row: K2tog. Bind off.

Sizes 12 mos and 3 yrs only: Next row: (Right Side). Sl1. K1. psso. Pat to last 3 sts. K2tog. P1.
Next row: P2tog. Pat to last 2 sts. P2togtbl. {11-14} sts.

Size 18 mos only: Next row: (Right Side). Sl1. K1. psso. Pat to last 3 sts. K2tog. P1. 11 sts.
Next row: Work even in pat.

Sizes 12 mos, 18 mos, 2 and 3 yrs only: Next row: (Right Side). Sl1. K1. psso. Pat to last 2 sts. K2tog.
Next row: P2tog. Pat to end of row.
Rep last 2 rows {2-2-1-3} time(s) more. {2-2-6-2} sts.

Size 2 yrs only: Next row: (Right Side). Pat to last 2 sts. K2tog.
Next row: P2tog. Pat to end of row. Rep last 2 rows once more. 2 sts.

Sizes 12 mos, 18 mos, 2 and 3 yrs only: Next row: (Right Side). K2tog. Bind off.

LEFT FRONT
With smaller needles, cast on 33 {42-45-45-48} sts.

Sizes 6 mos, 18 mos and 2 yrs only: 1st row: (Right Side). *K3. P3. Rep from * to last 3 sts. K3.
2nd row: *P1. K1. Rep from * to last st. P1.
Rep last 2 rows 4 times more.

Change to larger needles and proceed in pat as follows:
1st row: (Right Side). (Increase row). K3. P3. K3. (P3. K1. Inc 1 st in next st. K1. P3. K3) 2 {3-3} times. 35 {48-48} sts.
2nd row: *P1. K1. P1. K2. P6. K2. Rep from * to last 9 sts. (P1. K1) 4 times. P1.
3rd row: K3. P3. K3. (P2. Work 1st row of Panel Pat. P2. K3) 2 {3-3} times.
4th row: P1. K1. P1. K2. *Work 2nd row of Panel Pat. K2. P1. K1. P1. K2. Rep from * to last 9 sts. (P1. K1) 4 times. P1. Rep from * to end of row.
Panel Pat is now in position.

Sizes 12 mos and 3 yrs only: 1st row: (Right Side). *P3. K3. Rep from * to end of row.
2nd row: *P1. K1. Rep from * to end of row.
Rep last 2 rows 4 times more.

Change to larger needles and proceed in pat as follows:
1st row: (Right Side). (Increase row). (P3. K3) {1-0} time. (P3. K1. Inc 1 st in next st. K1. P3. K3) {3-4} times. {45-52} sts.
2nd row: *P1. K1. P1. K2. P6. K2. Rep from * to last {6-0} sts. (P1. K1) {3-0} times.
3rd row: (P3. K3) {1-0} time(s). (P2. Work 1st row of Panel Pat. P2. K3) 3 times.
4th row: *P1. K1. P1. K2. Work 2nd row of Panel Pat. K2. Rep from * to last {6-0} sts. (P1. K1) {3-0} times.
Panel Pat is now in position.

All Sizes: Cont even in pat until work from beg measures 6½ {7-7¾-8½-9¼}", ending with right side facing for next row.

Raglan shaping: Next row: Bind off 5 {5-7-7-7} sts. Pat to end of row. 30 {40-41-41-45} sts.
Work 1 row even in pat.
Next row: (Right Side). P1. Sl1. K1. psso. Pat to end of row.
Next row: Pat to last 2 sts. P1. K1.
Rep last 2 rows 11 {12-12-13-14} times more.
Next row: P1. Sl1. K1. psso. Pat to end of row. 17 {26-27-26-29} sts.

Neck shaping: Next row: (Wrong Side). Pat to last 6 {8-8-8-8} sts. **Turn.** Leave rem 6 {8-8-8-8} sts on a safety pin.
Next row: P1. Sl1. K1. psso. Pat to last 2 sts. K2tog.
Next row: P2tog. Pat to end of row.
Rep last 2 rows 0 {0-1-1-0} time(s) more. 8 {15-13-12-18} sts.

Size 6 mos only: Next row: (Right Side). P1. Sl1. K1. psso. Pat 3 sts. K2tog. 6 sts.
Next row: Work even in pat.
Next row: P1. Sl1. K1. psso. K1. K2tog. 4 sts.
Next row: P4.
Next row: Sl1. K1. psso. K2tog. 2 sts.
Next row: P2.
Next row: Sl1. K1. psso. Bind off.

Sizes 12 mos and 3 yrs only: Next row: (Right Side). P1. Sl1. K1. psso. Pat to last 2 sts. K2tog.
Next row: P2tog. Pat to last 2 sts. P2togtbl. {11-14} sts.

Size 18 mos only: Next row: (Right Side). P1. Sl1. K1. psso. Pat to last 2 sts. K2tog. 11 sts.
Next row: Work even in pat.

Sizes 12 mos, 18 mos, 2 and 3 yrs only: Next row: (Right Side). Sl1. K1. psso. Pat to last 2 sts. K2tog.
Next row: Pat to last 2 sts. P2togtbl.
Rep last 2 rows {2-2-1-3} time(s) more. {2-2-6-2} sts.

Size 2 yrs only: Next row: (Right Side). Sl1. K1. psso. Pat to end of row.
Next row: Pat to last 2 sts. P2togtbl.
Rep last 2 rows once more. 2 sts.

Sizes 12 mos, 18 mos, 2 and 3 yrs only: Next row: (Right Side). Sl1. K1. psso. Bind off.

SLEEVES

With smaller needles, cast on 45 {45-45-51-51} sts.

Sizes 6, 12 and 18 mos only: 1st row: (Right Side). *P3. K3. Rep from * to last 3 sts. P3.
2nd row: K1. *P1. K1. Rep from * to end of row.
Rep last 2 rows 4 times more.

Change to larger needles and proceed in pat as follows:
Next row: (Right Side). (Increase row). P3. K1. Inc 1 st in next st. K1. P3. (K3. P3. K1. Inc 1 st in next st. K1. P3) 3 times. 49 sts.
Next row: *K2. P6. K2. P1. K1. P1. Rep from * to last 10 sts. K2. P6. K2.
Next row: P2. Work 1st row of Panel Pat. P2. (K3. P2. Work 1st row of Panel pat. P2) 3 times.
Next row: *K2. Work 2nd row of Panel Pat. K2. P1. K1. P1. Rep from * to last 10 sts. K2. Work 2nd row of Panel Pat. K2.
Panel Pat is now in position.

Sizes 2 and 3 yrs only: 1st row: (Right Side). *K3. P3. Rep from * to last 3 sts. K3.
2nd row: P1. *K1. P1. Rep from * to end of row.
Rep last 2 rows 4 times more.

Change to larger needles and proceed in pat as follows:
Next row: (Right Side). (Increase row). (K3. P3. K1. Inc 1 st in next st. K1. P3) 4 times. K3. 55 sts.
Next row: P1. K1. P1. *K2. P6. K2. P1. K1. P1. Rep from * to end of row.
Next row: (K3. P2. Work 1st row of Panel Pat. P2) 4 times. K3.
Next row: P1. K1. P1. *K2. Work 2nd row of Panel Pat. K2. P1. K1. P1. Rep from * to end of row.
Panel Pat is now in position.

All Sizes: Keeping cont of Panel Pat, inc 1 st each end of needle on next and every following 4th row until there are 63 {65-69-71-73} sts, taking inc sts into pat.

Cont even in pat until work from beg measures 6 {7$\frac{1}{2}$-8-9-10}", ending with right side facing for next row.

Raglan shaping: Keeping cont of pat, bind off 5 {5-7-7-7} sts beg next 2 rows. 53 {55-55-57-59} sts.
Next row: P1. Sl1. K1. psso. Pat to last 3 sts. K2tog. P1.
Next row: K1. P1. Pat to last 2 sts. P1. K1.
Rep last 2 rows 14 {17-19-20-21} times more. 23 {19-15-15-15} sts.

Next row: (Right Side). P1. Sl1. K1. psso. Pat to last 3 sts. K2tog. P1.
Next row: K1. P2tog. Pat to last 3 sts. P2togtbl. K1.
Rep last 2 rows 2 {1-0-0-0} time(s) more.
Leave rem 11 sts on a st holder.

FINISHING

Neckband: Sew raglan seams.
With smaller needles and right side of work facing, K6 {8-8-8-8} from Right Front safety pin. Pick up and knit 8 {9-11-12-12} sts up Right Front neck edge. K11 from Right Sleeve st holder dec 3 sts evenly across. K26 {27-29-32-34} sts from Back st holder, dec 1 {2-2-1-3} st(s) evenly across. K11 from Left Sleeve st holder dec 3 sts evenly across. Pick up and knit 8 {9-11-12-12} sts down Left Front neck edge. K6 {8-8-8-8} from Left Front safety pin. 69 {75-81-87-87} sts.
Next row: (Wrong Side). P3. *K3. P3. Rep from * to end of row.
Next row: K1. *P1. K1. Rep from * to end of row.
Rep last 2 rows twice more. Bind off in pat.

Button Band: With smaller needles, cast on 7 sts.
1st row: (Right Side). K2. (P1. K1) twice. K1.
2nd row: (K1. P1) 3 times. K1.
Rep last 2 rows until band when slightly stretched, fits up Right Front to top of neckband, sewing in place as you work. Mark position for 5 buttons, having the top button ½" below neck edge, the bottom button ½" above lower edge and rem 3 buttons spaced evenly between.

Work Buttonhole Band as given for Button Band working buttonholes to correspond to button position as follows:
Next row: (Right Side). Rib 3. Bind off 2 sts. Rib to end of row.
Next row: Rib, casting on 2 sts over bound off sts. Bind off in ribbing.

Sew side and sleeve seams. Sew buttons to correspond to buttonholes.

Hat

Note: *Hat is sized for 6 mos, 12-18 mos and 2-3 yrs.*
With smaller needles, cast on 105 {**117**-129} sts.
1st row: (Right Side). P3. *K3. P3. Rep from * to end of row.
2nd row: K1. *P1. K1. Rep from * to end of row. Rep last 2 rows 8 times more.

Change to larger needles and proceed as follows:
1st row: (Right Side). (Increase row). P3. (K3. P3. K1. Inc 1 st in next st. K1. P3) 8 {**9**-10} times. K3. P3. 113 {**126**-139} sts.
Next row: (K1. P1) 3 times. *K2. P6. K2. P1. K1. P1. Rep from * to last 3 sts. K1. P1. K1.

Next row: P3. *K3. P2. Work 1st row of Panel Pat. P2. Rep from * to last 6 sts. K3. P3.
Next row: (K1. P1) 3 times. *K2. Work 2nd row of Panel Pat. K2. P1. K1. P1. Rep from * to last 3 sts. K1. P1. K1.
Panel Pat is now in position.

Cont even in pat until work from beg measures 7 {**8½**-8½}", ending with right side facing for next row.

Shape top: 1st row: P1. P2tog. *K3. P2tog. Work appropriate row of Panel Pat. P2tog. Rep from * to last 6 sts. K3. P2tog. P1. 95 {**106**-117} sts.
2nd row: K3. P1. K1. *K1. Work appropriate row of Panel Pat. (K1. P1) twice. Rep from * to last 2 sts. K2.
3rd row: P2tog. *K1. K2tog. P1. Work appropriate row of Panel Pat. P1. Rep from * to last 5 sts. K2tog. K1. P2tog. 84 {**94**-104} sts.
4th row: K1. P2. *K1. Work appropriate row of Panel Pat. K1. P2. Rep from * to last st. K1.
5th row: P1. *K2tog. P1. Work appropriate row of Panel Pat. P1. Rep from * to last 3 sts. K2tog. K1. 75 {**84**-93} sts. Draw yarn through rem sts and fasten securely. Sew back seam, reversing seam for cuff turn-back.

Pom-pom: Wind yarn around 4 fingers approx 100 times. Remove from fingers and tie tightly in center. Cut through each side of loops. Trim to a smooth round shape. Sew to top of Hat.

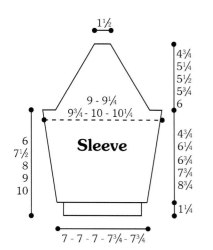

Sleeve

1½

4¾ 5¼ 5½ 5¾ 6

9 - 9¼
9¾ - 10 - 10¼

4¾ 6¼ 6¾ 7¾ 8¾

6 7½ 8 9 10

7 - 7 - 7 - 7¾ - 7¾

1¼

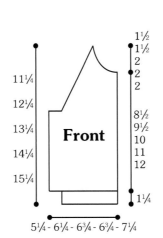

Front

1½ 1½ 2 2 2

11¼

12¼

13¼

14¼

15¼

8½ 9½ 10 11 12

1¼

5¼ - 6¼ - 6¾ - 6¾ - 7¼

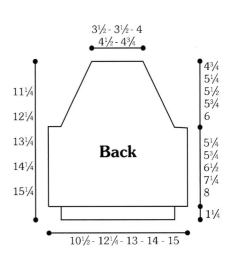

Back

3½ - 3½ - 4
4½ - 4¾

11¼

12¼

13¼

14¼

15¼

4¾ 5¼ 5½ 5¾ 6

5¼ 5¾ 6½ 7¼ 8

1¼

10½ - 12¼ - 13 - 14 - 15

21. Fishermen's Rib Jacket & Vest Intermediate

SIZES

Chest/bust measurement
Petite	28"
Small	30-32"
Medium	34-36"
Large	38-40"

Finished chest/bust
Petite	35½"
Small	38"
Medium	41"
Large	44"

Size Note: The instructions are written for Petite with sizes Small, Medium and Large in braces { }. Instructions will be easier to read if you circle all the numbers pertaining to your size. If only one number is given, it applies to all sizes.

MATERIALS

Worsted Weight Yarn: 3½ oz (223 yds/100g)

Sizes	P	S	M	L	
Jacket					
Dark Grey	**6**	**6**	**7**	**7**	balls
Vest					
Natural Mix	**3**	**4**	**4**	**5**	balls

Samples made with **Patons Classic Merino Wool.**

Size 7 (4.5 mm) knitting needles and one size 7 (4.5 mm) circular needle 36" long **or size needed for gauge.** Separating zipper.

GAUGE SWATCH

22 sts and 28 rows = 4" in rib pat.

STITCH GUIDE

> **yb** = take yarn to back of work.
> **yf** = take yarn to front of work.

JACKET
LEFT FRONT
** Cast on 49 {**53**-57-**61**} sts.

1st row: (Right Side). P1. *K3. P1. Rep from * to end of row.

2nd row: K2. P1. *K3. P1. Rep from * to last 2 sts. K2. These 2 rows form rib pat. **

Cont in rib pat until work from beg measures 12 {**12**-12-**12½**}", ending with right side facing for next row.

Shape Armhole: Cont in pat, bind off 4 {**4**-5-**5**} sts beg next row.

Work 1 row even in pat.
Dec 1 st at armhole edge on next 3 {**7**-9-**9**} rows, then every following alt row to 39 {**40**-42-**45**} sts.

Cont in rib pat until armhole measures 6 {**6½**-7-**7½**}", ending with **wrong side** facing for next row.

Neck shaping: Next row: Bind off 6 {**6**-7-**8**} sts. Pat to end of row.

Keeping cont of pat , dec 1 st at neck edge on next 9 {**9**-7-**7**} rows, then every following alt row to 21 {**22**-23-**24**} sts.

Work 1 row even in pat.

Shoulder shaping: Bind off 7 {**7**-8-**8**} sts beg next and following alt row.
Work 1 row even in pat.
Bind off rem 7 {**8**-7-**8**} sts.

RIGHT FRONT

Work from ** to ** as given for Left Front.

Cont in rib pat until work from beg measures same length as Left Front to beg of armhole shaping, ending with **wrong side** facing for next row.

Armhole shaping: Keeping cont of rib pat, bind off 4 {**4**-5-**5**} sts beg next row.
Dec 1 st at armhole edge on next 3 {**7**-9-**9**} rows, then every following alt row to 39 {**40**-42-**45**} sts.

Cont even in rib pat, until armhole measures same length as Left Front to beg of neck shaping, ending with right side facing for next row.

Neck shaping: Next row: Bind off 6 {**6**-7-**8**} sts. Pat to end of row.
Work 1 row even in pat.

Keeping cont of pat, dec 1 st at neck edge on next 9 {**9**-7-**7**} rows, then every following alt row to 21 {**22**-23-**24**} sts.

Shoulder shaping: Bind off 7 {**7**-8-**8**} sts beg next and following alt row.
Work 1 row even in pat.
Bind off rem 7 {**8**-7-**8**} sts.

BACK

Cast on 97 {**105**-113-**121**} sts.

Proceed in rib pat as given for Left Front until work from beg measures same as Front to beg of armhole shaping, ending with right side facing for next row.

Armhole shaping: Keeping cont of rib pat, bind off 4 {**4**-5-**5**} sts beg next 2 rows. Dec 1 st each end of next 3 {**7**-9-**9**} rows, then every following alt row to 77 {**79**-83-**89**} sts.

Cont even in pat until armhole measures same length as Front to beg of shoulder shaping, ending with right side facing for next row.

Shoulder shaping: Bind off 7 {**7**-8-**8**} sts beg next 4 rows. Bind off 7 {**8**-7-**8**} sts beg next 2 rows. Bind off rem 35 {**35**-37-**41**} sts.

SLEEVES

Cast on 49 {**53**-53-**57**} sts.

Proceed in rib pat as given for Left Front, inc 1 st each end of needle on 5th and every following 4th {**6th**-4th-**4th**} row to 55 {**83**-63-**67**} sts, then every following 6th {**8th**-6th-**6th**} row to 83 {**87**-93-**99**} sts, taking inc sts into pat.

Cont even in rib pat until Sleeve from beg measures 16½ {**17**-17½ -**18½**}", ending with right side facing for next row.

Shape top: Bind off 4 {**4**-5-**5**} sts beg next 2 rows. Dec 1 st each end of needle on next and every following alt row 3 times. 67 {**71**-75-**81**} sts.
Work 1 row even in pat. Bind off.

FINISHING

Pin garment pieces to measurements, cover with a damp cloth and allow to dry.

Sew shoulder seams.

Collar: Cast on 85 {**89**-93-**101**} sts.
1st row: K1. *P1. K1. Rep from * to end of row.
2nd row: P1. *K1. P1. Rep from * to end of row.
3rd row: K1. *P1. K1. Rep from * 30 {**32**-33-**36**} times. P1. yb. Sl1. yf. Slip st back onto left-hand needle. **Turn.**
4th row: *K1. P1. Rep from * 19 {**21**-21-**23**} times. yb. Sl1. yf. Slip st back onto left-hand needle. Turn.
5th row: *K1. P1. Rep from * 14 {**16**-16-**18**} times. yb. Sl1. yf. Slip st back onto left-hand needle. Turn.
6th row: *K1. P1. Rep from * 9 {**11**-11-**13**} times. yb. Sl1. yf. Slip st back onto left-hand needle. Turn.
7th row: Rib to end of row.
Work a further 18 rows in (K1. P1) ribbing. Bind off in ribbing.
Sew cast on edge of collar to neck edge. Sew in sleeves. Sew side and sleeve seams. Sew zipper in position, leaving collar free.

VEST

LEFT FRONT

Work as for Left Front of Jacket from ** to **.
Cont in rib pat until work from beg measures 12½ {**12½**-12½-**13**}", ending with right side facing for next row.

Armhole shaping: Keeping cont of pat bind off 4 {**4**-5-**5**} sts beg next row.
Work 1 row even in pat.
Dec 1 st at armhole edge on next 3 {**7**-9-**9**} rows, then every following alt row to 39 {**40**-42-**45**} sts.

Cont even in pat until armhole measures 4½ {**5**-5½-**6**}", ending with **wrong side** facing for next row.

Neck shaping: Dec 1 st at neck edge on next and every following row to 21 {**22**-23-**24**} sts.
Cont even in pat until armhole measures 7½ {**8**-8½-**9**}", ending with right side facing for next row.

Shoulder shaping: Bind off 7 {**7**-8-**8**} sts beg next and following alt row.
Work 1 row even in pat.
Bind off rem 7 {**8**-7-**8**} sts.

RIGHT FRONT

Work as for Left Front of Jacket from ** to **.

Cont in rib pat until work from beg measures 12½ {**12½**-12½-**13**}", ending with **wrong side** facing for next row.

Armhole shaping: Keeping cont of pat bind off 4 {**4**-5-**5**} sts beg next row.
Work 1 row even in pat.
Dec 1 st at armhole edge on next 3 {**7**-9-**9**} rows, then every following alt row to 39 {**40**-42-**45**} sts.

Cont even in pat until armhole measures 4½ {**5**-5½-**6**}", ending with right side facing for next row.

Neck shaping: Dec 1 st at neck edge on next and every following row to 21 {**22**-23-**24**} sts.
Cont even in pat until armhole measures 7½ {**8**-8½-**9**}", ending with **wrong side** facing for next row.

Shoulder shaping: Bind off 7 {**7**-8-**8**} sts beg next and following alt row.
Work 1 row even in pat.
Bind off rem 7 {**8**-7-**8**} sts.

BACK

Cast on 97 {**105**-113-**121**} sts.
Proceed in rib pat as given for Left Front until work from beg measures same length as Front to beg of armhole shaping, ending with right side facing for next row.

Armhole shaping: Keeping cont of pat bind off 4 {**4**-5-**5**} sts beg next 2 rows.
Dec 1 st each end of needle on next 3 {**7**-9-**9**} rows, then every following alt row to 77 {**79**-83-**89**} sts.

Cont even in pat until armhole measures same length as Front to beg of shoulder shaping, ending with right side facing for next row.

Shoulder shaping: Bind off 7 {**7**-8-**8**} sts beg next 4 rows.
Bind off 7 {**8**-7-**8**} sts beg next 2 rows. Bind off rem 35 {**35**-37-**41**} sts.

FINISHING

Pin garment pieces to measurements, cover with a damp cloth and allow to dry.

Sew shoulder seams.

Front edging: With right side of work facing and circular needle, pick up and knit 60 {**60**-60-**65**} sts up Right Front edge, 27 {**29**-31-**35**} sts up Right Front neck edge, 33 {**33**-35-**37**} sts across Back neck edge, 27 {**29**-31-**35**} sts down Left Front neck edge and 60 {**60**-60-**65**} sts down Left Front edge. 207 {**211**-217-**237**} sts. Bind off knitwise (**wrong side**).

Armhole edging: With right side of work facing, pick up and knit 76 {**80**-86-**90**} sts along armhole edge. Bind off knitwise (**wrong side**).
Sew side seams. Sew zipper in position under front edging.

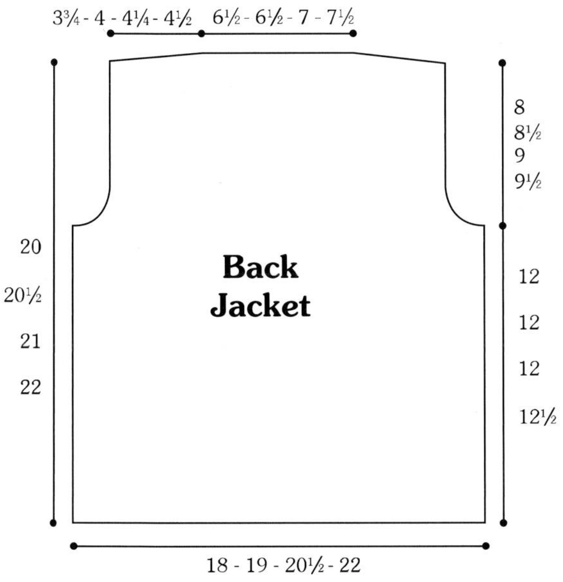
3¾ - 4 - 4¼ - 4½
6½ - 6½ - 7 - 7½
Back
Jacket
20
20½
21
22
8
8½
9
9½
12
12
12
12½
18 - 19 - 20½ - 22

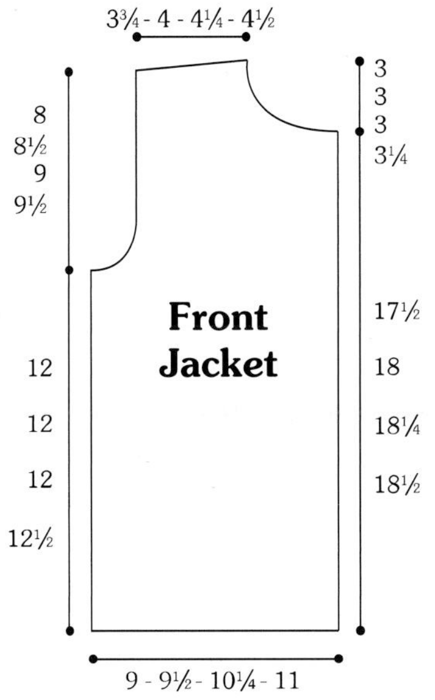
3¾ - 4 - 4¼ - 4½
Front
Jacket
8
8½
9
9½
12
12
12
12½
3
3
3
3¼
17½
18
18¼
18½
9 - 9½ - 10¼ - 11

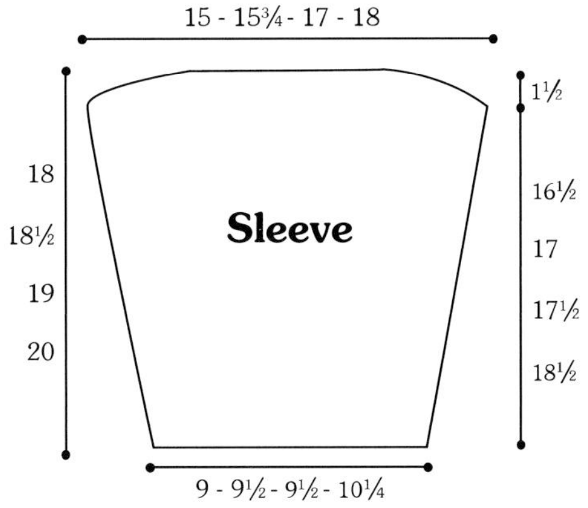
15 - 15¾ - 17 - 18
Sleeve
18
18½
19
20
1½
16½
17
17½
18½
9 - 9½ - 9½ - 10¼

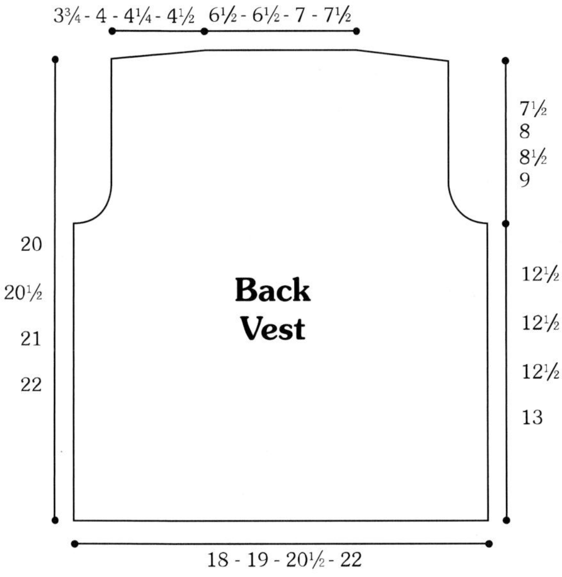
3¾ - 4 - 4¼ - 4½
6½ - 6½ - 7 - 7½
Back
Vest
20
20½
21
22
7½
8
8½
9
12½
12½
12½
13
18 - 19 - 20½ - 22

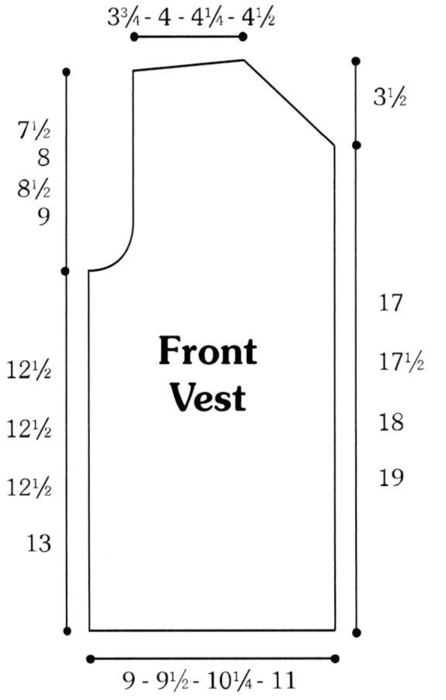
3¾ - 4 - 4¼ - 4½
Front
Vest
7½
8
8½
9
12½
12½
12½
13
3½
17
17½
18
19
9 - 9½ - 10¼ - 11

22. Easy Stripes Garter Sweater

Easy

SIZES

Chest/Bust measurement

Petite	28"
Small	30-32"
Medium	34-36"
Large	38-40"

Finished chest/bust

Petite	40"
Small	43"
Medium	46"
Large	49"

Size Note: *The instructions are written for Petite with sizes Small, Medium and Large in braces { }. Instructions will be easier to read if you circle all the numbers pertaining to your size. If only one number is given, it applies to all sizes.*

MATERIALS

Worsted Weight Yarn: 3½ oz (223 yds/100g)

Sizes	P	S	M	L	
Russet	**2**	**3**	**3**	**4**	**balls**
Paprika	**3**	**3**	**4**	**4**	**balls**
Green	**2**	**2**	**2**	**3**	**balls**
Gold	**1**	**1**	**2**	**2**	**ball(s)**

Sample made with **Patons Classic Merino Wool.**

Sizes 6 (4 mm) and 7 (4.5 mm) knitting needles **or size needed for gauge.** 2 st holders.

GAUGE SWATCH

20 sts and 26 rows = 4" with larger needles in stocking st.

FRONT

With Russet and smaller needles cast on 99 {107**-113-**121**} sts.
1st row: (Right Side). K1. *P1. K1. Rep from * to end of row.
2nd row: P1. *K1. P1. Rep from * to end of row.
Rep last 2 rows (K1. P1) ribbing for 1½", ending on a 2nd row and inc 1 st in center of last row. 100 {**108**-114-**122**} sts.

Change to larger needles and proceed in stripe pat as follows:
1st row: With Russet, knit.
2nd row: Purl.
3rd row: With Paprika, knit.
4th row: Purl.
5th to 8th rows: Rep 3rd and 4th rows twice.
9th row: With Green, knit.
10th row: Purl.
11th and 12th rows: As 9th and 10th rows.
13th and 14th rows: With Gold, knit.
15th and 16th rows: As 1st and 2nd rows.
17th to 20th rows: Rep 3rd and 4th rows twice.
21st and 22nd rows: With Green, knit.
23rd to 26th rows: Rep 1st and 2nd rows twice.
27th row: With Gold, knit.
28th row: Purl.
29th and 30th rows: With Paprika, knit.
31st and 32nd rows: As 9th and 10th rows.
33rd and 34th rows: With Russet, knit.
35th to 38th rows: Rep 3rd and 4th rows twice.
39th and 40th rows: With Gold, knit.
41st and 42nd rows: With Green, knit.
These 42 rows form stripe pat.**

Cont in pat until work from beg measures 22½ {23-23¾-**24**}", ending with right side facing for next row.

Neck shaping: Next row: Pat across 45 {**49**-51-**54**} sts (neck edge). **Turn.** Leave rem sts on a spare needle.

Work 1 row even in pat.
Dec 1 st at neck edge on next 7 {**11**-9-**7**} rows, then every following alt row to 34 {**36**-38-**41**} sts.
Work 3 rows even in pat.

Shoulder shaping: Bind off 11 {**12**-13-**14**} sts beg next and following alt row.
Work 1 row even in pat.
Bind off rem 12 {**12**-12-**13**} sts.

With right side of work facing, slip first 10 {**10**-12-**14**} sts onto a st holder.
Join yarn to rem 45 {**49**-51-**54**} sts and pat to end of row.
Work 1 row even in pat.
Dec 1 st at neck edge on next 7 {**11**-9-**7**} rows, then every following alt row to 34 {**36**-38-**41**} sts.
Work 4 rows even in pat.

Shoulder shaping: Bind off 11 {**12**-13-**14**} sts beg next and following alt row.
Work 1 row even in pat.
Bind off rem 12 {**12**-12-**13**} sts.

BACK

Work from ** to ** as given for Front.

Cont in pat until work from beg measures same length as Front to beg of shoulder shaping, ending with right side facing for next row.

Shoulder shaping: Bind off 11 {**12**-13-**14**} sts beg next 4 rows.

Bind off 12 {**12**-12-**13**} sts beg next 2 rows.
Leave rem 32 {**36**-38-**40**} sts on a st holder.

SLEEVES

With Russet and smaller needles, cast on 57 {**59**-63-**65**} sts.
Work 1½" in (K1. P1) ribbing as given for Front, ending on a 2nd row and inc 1 st in center of last row. 58 {**60**-64-**66**} sts.

Change to larger needles and proceed in stripe pat as given for Front, inc 1 st at each end of needle on next and every following 4th row to 62 {**68**-68-**76**} sts, then every following 6th row to 88 {**94**-98-**104**} sts.

Cont even in stripe pat until Sleeve from beg measures 16½ {**17½**-18-**19**}", ending with right side facing for next row. Bind off.

FINISHING

Pin garment pieces to measurements, cover with a damp cloth and allow to dry.

Neckband: Sew right shoulder seam. With right side of work facing, Russet and smaller needles, pick up and knit 18 {**19**-20-**21**} sts down Left Front neck edge. Knit across 10 {**10**-12-**14**} sts from Front st holder. Pick up and knit 18 {**19**-20-**21**} sts up Right Front neck edge. Knit across 32 {**36**-38-**40**} sts from Back st holder, dec 1 st in center. 77 {**83**-89-**95**} sts.

Beg and ending with a 2nd row, work 1" in (K1. P1) ribbing as given for Front. Bind off loosely in ribbing. Sew left shoulder and neckband seam. Place markers on Front and Back side edges 9 {**9½**-10-**10½**}" down from shoulder seams. Sew in sleeves between markers. Sew side and sleeve seams.

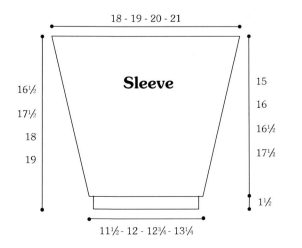

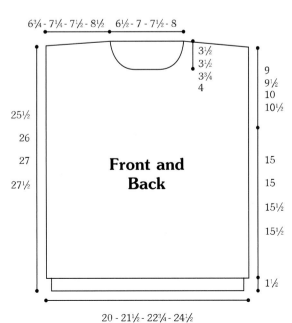

23. From The Sea Pullovers

Intermediate

SIZES

Chest measurement

4	23"
6	25"
8	26½"
10	28"

Finished chest

4	28"
6	30"
8	32"
10	34"

Size Note: *Instructions are written for size 4, with sizes 6, 8, and 10 in braces { }. Instructions will be easier to read if you circle all the numbers pertaining to your size. If only one number is given, it applies to all sizes.*

MATERIALS

Sport Weight Yarn: 1¾ oz (136 yds/50 g)

Sizes	4	6	8	10	
Boat Version					
Blue	5	6	7	8	balls
Beige	1	1	1	1	ball
White	1	1	1	1	ball
Fish Version					
Bright Blue	5	6	7	8	balls
Pale Blue	1	1	1	1	ball
White	1	1	1	1	ball

Samples made with **Patons Grace.**

Sizes 3 (3.25 mm) and 5 (3.75 mm) knitting needles **or size needed for gauge.** Size 3 (3.25 mm) circular knitting needle 24" long. 3 stitch holders.

GAUGE SWATCH
24 sts and 32 rows = 4" with larger needles in stocking st.

BACK
With Beige or Pale Blue and smaller needles, cast on 82 {86**-90-**98**} sts.

1st row: (Right Side). *K2. P2. Rep from * to last 2 sts. K2.

2nd row: *P2. K2. Rep from * to last 2 sts. P2. Break Beige or Pale Blue.

With Blue or Bright Blue, rep last 2 rows (K2. P2) ribbing 3 times more (8 rows in all), inc 2 {**4**-6-**4**} sts evenly across last row. 84 {**90**-96-**102**} sts.

Change to larger needles and proceed in stocking st until work from beg measures 9 {**10**-11-**12**}" ending with right side facing for next row.

Shape raglans: Bind off 2 sts beg next 2 rows. 80 {**86**-92-**98**} sts.

Next row: (Right Side). K2. K2tog. Knit to last 4 sts. Sl1. K1. psso. K2.

Work 3 rows even.

Rep last 4 rows 1 {**2**-2-**2**} time(s) more. 76 {**80**-86-**92**} sts.

Next row: (Right Side). K2. K2tog. Knit to last 4 sts. Sl1. K1. psso. K2.

Next row: Purl.**

Rep last 2 rows until there are 36 {**38**-40-**42**} sts, ending with a purl row. Leave rem sts on a st holder.

FRONT
Work from ** to ** as given for Back.

Rep last 2 rows until there are 70 {**74**-78-**80**} sts, ending with a purl row.

Shape placket opening: 1st row: (Right Side). K2. K2tog. K31 {**33**-35-**36**} (placket opening). **Turn.** Leave rem sts on a spare needle.

2nd row: Purl.

3rd row: K2. K2tog. Knit to end of row.

4th row: Purl.

Rep last 2 rows until there are 26 {**28**-30-**31**} sts, ending with a purl row.

Shape neck: 1st row: (Right Side). K2. K2tog. K15 {**16**-18-**18**} (neck edge). **Turn.** Leave rem 7 {**8**-8-**9**} sts on a safety pin.

2nd row: P2togtbl. Purl to end of row.

3rd row: K2. K2tog. Knit to last 2 sts. Sl1. K1. psso.

Sizes 6, 8 and 10 only: Rep last 2 rows once more.

All Sizes: Next row: Purl.

Next row: K2. K2tog. Knit to last 2 sts. Sl1. K1. psso. Rep last 2 rows until there are 5 sts, ending with a purl row.

Next row: K1. K2tog. Sl1. K1. psso.

Next row: P3.

Next row: K1. K2tog.

Next row: P2.

Next row: K2tog. Fasten off.

With right side of work facing, join Blue or Bright Blue to rem 35 {**37**-39-**40**} sts.

1st row: Knit to last 4 sts. Sl1. K1. psso. K2.

2nd row: Purl.

Rep last 2 rows until there are 26 {**28**-30-**31**} sts, ending with a purl row.

Shape neck: 1st row: (Right Side). K7 {**8**-8-**9**} (neck edge). Slip these sts onto a safety pin. Knit to last 4 sts. Sl1. K1. psso. K2.

2nd row: Purl to last 2 sts. P2tog.

3rd row: K2tog. Knit to last 4 sts. Sl1. K1. psso. K2.

Sizes 6, 8 and 10 only: Rep last 2 rows once more.

All Sizes: Next row: Purl.

Next row: K2tog. Knit to last 4 sts. Sl1. K1. psso. K2. Rep last 2 rows until there are 5 sts, ending with a purl row.

Next row: K2tog. Sl1. K1. psso. K1.

Next row: P3.

Next row: Sl1. K1. psso. K1.

Next row: P2.

Next row: Sl1. K1. psso. Fasten off.

SLEEVES
With Beige or Pale Blue and smaller needles, cast on 42 {**42**-46-**46**} sts.

Work 2 rows in (K2. P2) ribbing as given for Back. Break Beige or Pale Blue.

With Blue or Bright Blue, work a further 6 rows in (K2. P2) ribbing, inc 4 {**6**-4-**6**} sts evenly across last row. 46 {**48**-50-**52**} sts.

Change to larger needles and proceed in stocking st inc 1 st each end of needle on 7th and every following 6th row until there are 68 {**74**-78-**84**} sts.

Cont even until work from beg measures 10½ {**12½**-14-**16½**}", ending with right side facing for next row.

Shape raglans: Bind off 2 sts beg next 2 rows. 64 {**70**-74-**80**} sts.
1st row: K2. K2tog. Knit to last 4 sts. Sl1. K1. psso. K2.
2nd row: P2. P2togtbl. Purl to last 4 sts. P2tog. P2.
3rd row: As 1st row.
4th row: Purl.
Rep last 4 rows 1 {**2**-1-**2**} time(s) more. 52 {**52**-62-**62**} sts.

Next row: K2. K2tog. Knit to last 4 sts. Sl1. K1. psso. K2.
Next row: Purl.
Rep last 2 rows until there are 10 {**10**-12-**12**} sts, ending with a purl row. Leave rem sts on a st holder.

KANGAROO POCKET

Note: When working from chart, wind small balls of the colors to be used, one for each separate area of color in the design. Start new colors at appropriate points. To change colors, twist the two colors around each other where they meet, on **wrong side**, to avoid a hole. Work small areas of color in duplicate stitch.

With Blue or Bright Blue and larger needles, cast on 59 {**59**-65-**65**} sts.
Work Chart XV for Boat Version or Chart XVI for Fish Version in stocking st to end of chart, reading **knit** rows from **right** to left and **purl** rows from **left** to right, noting dec rows will be worked as follows: K2. K2tog. Knit to last 4 sts. Sl1. K1. psso. K2.
Bind off rem 31 {**31**-33-**33**} sts. *Charts XV and XVI are shown on pages 114 and 115.*

Neck edging: Sew raglan seams. With right side of work facing, Blue or Bright Blue and circular needle, K7 {**8**-8-**9**} from Right Front safety pin. Pick up and knit 12 {**12**-14-**14**} sts up Right Front neck edge. K10 {**10**-12-**12**} from right sleeve st holder, dec 2 sts evenly across. K36 {**38**-40-**42**} from Back st holder, dec 4 sts evenly across. K10 {**10**-12-**12**} from left sleeve st holder, dec 2 sts evenly across. Pick up and knit 12 {**12**-14-**14**} sts down Left Front neck edge. K7 {**8**-8-**9**} from Left Front safety pin. 86 {**90**-100-**104**} sts. **Do not** join. Working back and forth across needle in rows, proceed as follows:
Next row: (Wrong Side). Knit.
With White, knit 2 rows.
With Beige or Pale Blue, knit 2 rows. Bind off.

Placket edging: With right side of work facing, smaller needles and Blue or Bright Blue, pick up and knit 36 sts evenly around Placket opening (including sides of neck edging). Bind off knitwise (**wrong side**).

Sew Pocket in position to Front as illustrated. Sew side and sleeve seams.

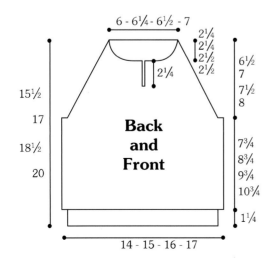

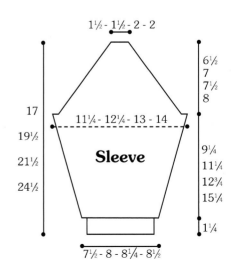

Chart XV

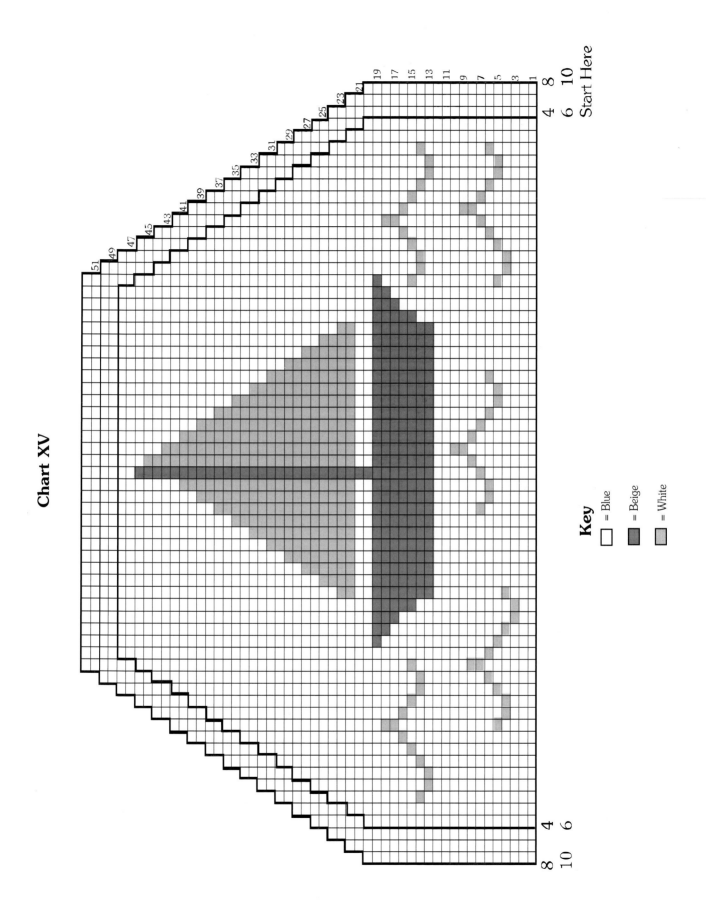

Key

☐ = Blue

■ = Beige

▨ = White

Chart XVI

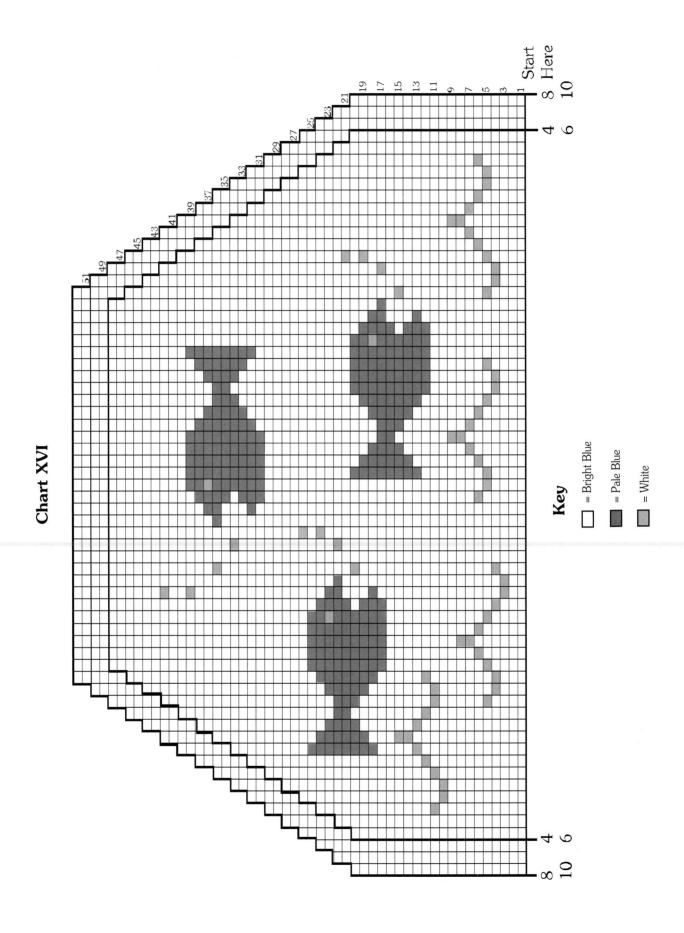

Key

☐ = Bright Blue

■ = Pale Blue

▨ = White

23

24. Superstar and Sweetheart

Intermediate

SIZES

Chest measurement

4	23"
6	25"
8	26½"

Finished chest

4	28"
6	31"
8	33"

Size Note: Instructions are written for size 4, with sizes 6 and 8 in braces { }. Instructions will be easier to read if you circle all the numbers pertaining to your size. If only one number is given, it applies to all sizes.

MATERIALS

Sport Weight Yarn: 1¾ oz (133 yds/50 g)

Sizes	4	6	8	
Star Version				
Aqua	5	5	6	balls
Blue	1	1	1	ball
Heart Version				
Pink	5	5	6	balls
Fuchsia	1	1	1	ball

Samples made with **Patons Astra.**

Size 5 (3.75 mm) knitting needles **or size needed for gauge.** 2 stitch holders.

GAUGE SWATCH

24 sts and 32 rows = 4" in stocking st.

BACK

With Aqua (for Him) or Pink (for Her) cast on 82 {90**-98} sts.
***Work 4 rows stocking st.
Next row: K2. *P2. K2. Rep from * to end of row.
Next row: P2. *K2. P2. Rep from * to end of row.***
Rep last 2 rows twice more inc 3 {**3**-1} st(s) evenly across last row. 85 {**93**-99} sts.**
Work 50 {**58**-70} rows stocking st, thus ending with right side facing for next row.

Shape armholes: Bind off 6 {**7**-7} sts beg next 2 rows. 73 {**79**-85} sts.
Work 50 {**54**-58} rows even, thus ending with right side facing for next row.
Shape shoulders: Bind off 6 {**7**-7} sts beg next 4 rows then 6 {**6**-8} sts beg following 2 rows. Leave rem 37 {**39**-41} sts on a st holder.

FRONT

Note: When working from chart, wind small balls of the colors to be used, one for each separate area of color in the design. Start new colors at appropriate points. To change colors, twist the 2 colors around each other where they meet, on **wrong side,** to avoid a hole. Work small areas of color in duplicate st.

Work from ** to ** as given for Back.
Work 6 {**14**-26} rows stocking st, thus ending with right side facing for next row.
Work Chart XVII for Star Version or Chart XVIII for Heart Version to end of chart. *(Chart XVII is shown on page 122. Chart XVIII is shown on page 123.)*

With Aqua (for Him) or Pink (for Her), work 2 {2-4} rows even.

Neck shaping: Next row: K26 {**29**-32} (neck edge). **Turn.** Leave rem sts on a spare needle.

Dec 1 st at neck edge on next 4 rows, then on every following alt row to 18 {**20**-22} sts.

Work 5 {**7**-9} rows even, thus ending with right side facing for next row.

Shape shoulder: Bind off 6 {**7**-7} sts beg next and following alt row. Bind off rem 6 {**6**-8} sts.

With right side facing slip center 21 sts onto a st holder. Join yarn to rem sts and knit to end of row.

Dec 1 st at neck edge on next 4 rows, then on every following alt row to 18 {**20**-22} sts.

Work 6 {**8**-10} rows even, thus ending with **wrong side** facing for next row.

Shape shoulder: Bind off 6 {**7**-7} sts beg next and following alt row. Bind off rem 6 {**6**-8} sts.

SLEEVES

With Aqua (for Him) or Pink (for Her) cast on 42 {**42**-46} sts.

Work from *** to *** as given for Back.

Rep last 2 rows twice more inc 5 {**7**-7} sts evenly across last row. 47 {**49**-53} sts.

Proceed in stocking st inc 1 st at each end of needle on 5th and every following 2nd {**2nd**-4th} row to 61 {**63**-91} sts.

Sizes 4 and 6 only: Inc 1 st each end of needle on every following 4th row to 79 {**85**} sts.

All Sizes: Cont even until Sleeve from beg measures 9½ {**11**-13}", ending with right side facing for next row. Place marker at each end of last row. Work a further 8 rows even. Bind off.

FINISHING

Neckband: Sew right shoulder seam. With right side of work facing and Aqua (for Him) or Pink (for Her), pick up and knit 20 {**21**-24} sts down Left Front neck edge. K21 from Front st holder dec 2 sts evenly across. Pick up and knit 20 {**21**-24} sts up Right Front neck edge. K37 {**39**-41} from Back st holder dec 2 sts evenly across. 94 {**98**-106} sts.

1st row: (**Wrong Side**). *P2. K2. Rep from * to last 2 sts. P2.

2nd row: *K2. P2. Rep from * to last 2 sts. K2.

Rep last 2 rows twice more, then 1st row once. Work 4 rows stocking st. Bind off.

Sew left shoulder and neckband seam, reversing seam on neckband for rolled edge.

Sew in sleeves placing rows above markers along bound off sts of Front and Back to form square armholes. Sew side and sleeve seams, allowing lower edges to curl.

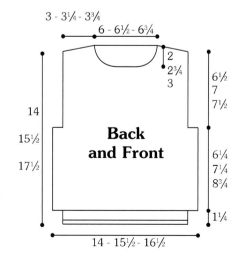

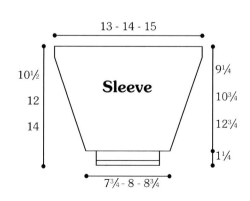

Chart XVII

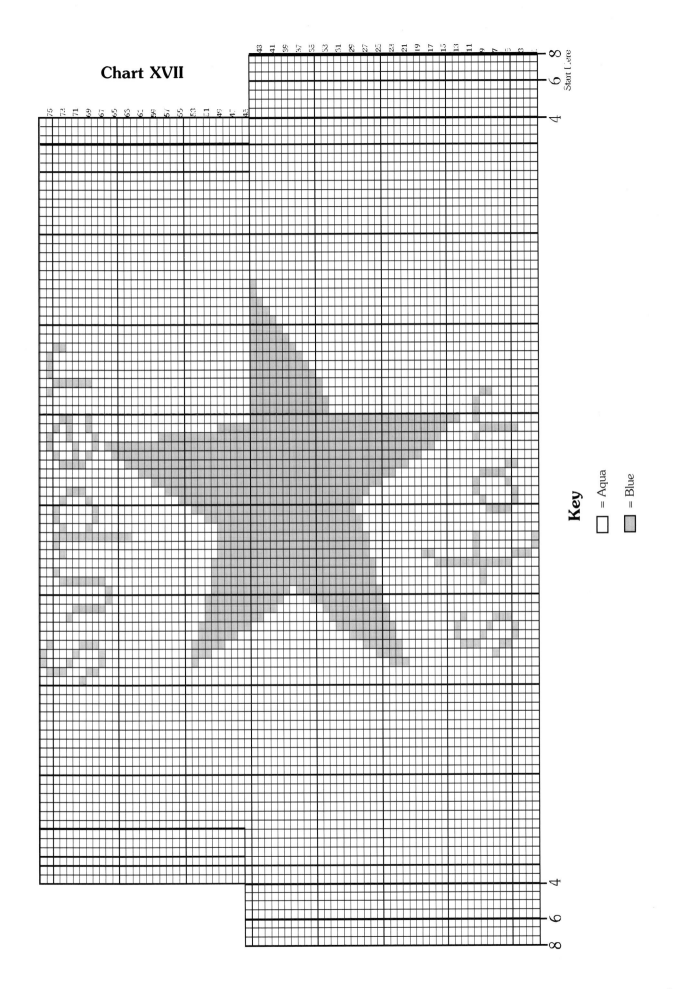

Key

☐ = Aqua

▨ = Blue

122

Chart XVIII

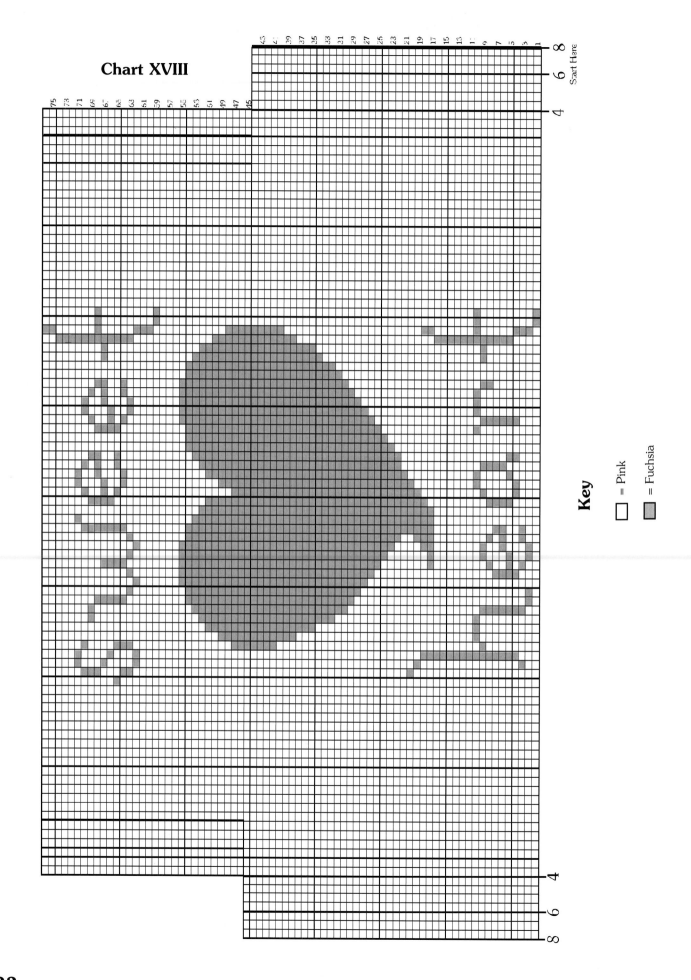

Key

☐ = Pink

▨ = Fuchsia

123

25. Sporty Zip Neck

SIZES

Chest measurement

2	21"
4	23"
6	25"
8	26½"

Finished chest

2	28"
4	30"
6	33"
8	35"

Size Note: Instructions are written for size 2, with sizes 4, 6 and 8 in braces { }. Instructions will be easier to read if you circle all the numbers pertaining to your size. If only one number is given, it applies to all sizes.

MATERIALS

Sport Weight Yarn: 1¾ oz (133 yds/50 g)

Sizes	2	4	6	8	
Girl's Version					
Red	4	5	6	7	balls
Yellow	1	1	1	1	ball
Bright Blue	1	1	1	1	ball
Boy's Version					
Bright Blue	4	5	6	7	balls
Yellow	1	1	1	1	ball
Green	1	1	1	1	ball

Samples made with **Patons Astra.**

Sizes 3 (3.25 mm) and 5 (3.75 mm) knitting needles **or size needed for gauge.** 4 st holders. Zipper. 1 yard of elastic ½" wide.

GAUGE SWATCH

24 sts and 32 rows = 4" with larger needles in stocking st.

BACK

With Yellow and smaller needles, cast on 85 {91-99-**105**} sts.

Work 12 rows in reverse stocking st. Break Yellow.

Next row: (Right Side). *With Red (for Her) or Bright Blue (for Him), pick up st from cast on row. Knit next st from needle and picked up st tog. Rep from * to end of row.

Next row: Knit.

Change to larger needles and proceed in pat as follows:

1st row: (Right Side). K1. *P1. K1. Rep from * to end of row.

2nd row: Knit.

These 2 rows form pat.******

Cont in pat until work from folded lower edge measures 9 {**10½**-11-**12**}", ending with right side facing for next row.

Armhole shaping: Bind off 7 {**7**-9-**9**} sts beg next 2 rows. 71 {**77**-81-**87**} sts.

Cont in pat until work from beg measures 15 {**17**-18-**19½**}", ending with right side facing for next row.

Shape shoulders: Bind off 23 {**26**-28-**31**} sts beg next 2 rows. Leave rem 25 sts on a st holder.

Pocket Lining

With Yellow and larger needles, cast on 41 {**41**-55-**55**} sts and work 12 rows in stocking st, thus ending with right side facing for next row. Leave these sts on a st holder.

FRONT

Work from ****** to ****** as given for Back.

Cont in pat until work from folded lower edge measures 2 {**3**-3-**4**}", ending with right side facing for next row.

Divide for Pocket: Next row: Pat across 22 {**25**-22-**25**} sts. With Yellow, K41 {**41**-55-**55**} from Pocket Lining. Leave next 41 {**41**-55-**55**} sts on a st holder. With Red (for Her) or Bright Blue (for Him), pat across 22 {**25**-22-**25**} sts.

Next row: With Red (for Her) or Bright Blue (for Him), pat across 22 {**25**-22-**25**} sts. With Yellow, P41 {**41**-55-**55**}. With Red (for Her) or Bright Blue (for Him), pat across 22 {**25**-22-**25**} sts.

Cont as established until 53 {**57**-61-**61**} rows in total have been worked.

Next row: (Wrong Side). With Red (for Her) or Bright Blue (for Him), K22 {**25**-22-**25**}. Bind off 41 {**41**-55-**55**} sts. With Red (for Her) or Bright Blue (for Him), K22 {**25**-22-**25**}. Break Yellow.

With right side of work facing, join Red (for Her) or Bright Blue (for Him) to center rem sts. Pat across 41 {**41**-55-**55**} sts.

Work a further 53 {**57**-61-**61**} rows in pat, thus ending with right side facing for next row. Break yarn. Leave these sts on a spare needle.

Joining row: Next row: (Right Side). With Red (for Her) or Bright Blue (for Him), pat across 22 {**25**-22-**25**} sts. Pat 41 {**41**-55-**55**} sts from st holder. Pat to end of row.

Work 1 row even in pat.

Divide for Zipper opening: Next row: Pat across 42 {**45**-49-**52**} sts. **Turn.** Leave rem sts on spare needle.

Cont in pat on these 42 {**45**-49-**52**} sts until work from beg measures same length as Back to armhole shaping, ending with right side facing for next row.

Armhole shaping: Next row: Bind off 7 {**7**-9-**9**} sts. Pat to end of row. 35 {**38**-40-**43**} sts.

Cont in pat until work from beg measures 13 {**15**-15½-**17**}", ending with right side facing for next row.

Neck shaping: Next row: Pat to last 7 sts. **Turn.** Leave rem 7 sts on a st holder.

Work 1 row even in pat.

Keeping cont of pat, dec 1 st at neck edge on next 4 rows, then on following alt row once. 23 {**26**-28-**31**} sts.

Cont even in pat until Front from beg measures same length as Back to shoulder, ending with right side facing for next row. Bind off.

With right side of work facing, slip first st from spare needle onto a safety pin, join Red (for Her) or Bright Blue (for Him) to rem sts and pat to end of row.

Cont in pat on these 42 {**45**-49-**52**} sts until work from beg measures same length as Back to armhole shaping, ending with **wrong side** facing for next row.

Armhole shaping: Next row: Bind off 7 {**7**-9-**9**} sts. Pat to end of row. 35 {**38**-40-**43**} sts.

Cont in pat until work from beg measures 13 {**15**-15½-**17**}", ending with **wrong side** facing for next row.

Neck shaping: Next row: Pat to last 7 sts. **Turn.** Leave rem 7 sts on a st holder.
Keeping cont of pat, dec 1 st at neck edge on next 4 rows, then on following alt row once. 23 {**26**-28-**31**} sts. Cont even in pat until Front from beg measures same length as Back to shoulder, ending with **wrong side** facing for next row. Bind off.

SLEEVES

With smaller needles and Yellow, cast on 51 {**51**-55-**55**} sts.
Work 12 rows in reverse stocking st. Break Yellow.
Next row: (Right Side). *With Red (for Her) or Bright Blue (for Him), pick up st from cast on row. Knit next st from needle and picked up st tog. Rep from * to end of row.
Next row: Knit.
Change to larger needles and proceed in pat as given for Back, inc 1 st each end of needle on next and every following 4th row to 73 {**79**-85-**91**} sts.
With Red (for Her) or Bright Blue (for Him), cont even in stocking st until Sleeve from folded lower edge measures 8 {**9½**-10½-**12**}", ending with right side facing for next row. Place markers at each end of last row.
Work 10 {**10**-12-**12**} rows even in pat. Bind off.

FLAP

With Bright Blue (for Her) or Green (for Him) and larger needles, cast on 41 {**41**-55-**55**} sts. Work 2" in pat as given for Back, ending with **wrong side** facing for next row.
Next row: Knit to last 10 {**10**-17-**17**} sts. yf. Sl1. yb. **Turn.** Sl1. Leave rem 10 {**10**-17-**17**} sts on spare needle.
Next row: Pat to last 10 {**10**-17-**17**} sts. yf. Sl1. yb. **Turn.** Sl1. Leave rem 10 {**10**-17-**17**} sts on spare needle. 21 sts.
Next row: K18. yf. Sl1. yb. **Turn.**
Next row: Sl1. Pat 15 sts. yf. Sl1. yb. **Turn.**
Next row: Sl1. K13. yf. Sl1. yb. **Turn.**
Next row: Sl1. Pat 11 sts. yf. Sl1. yb. **Turn.**
Next row: Sl1. K9. yf. Sl1. yb. **Turn.**
Next row: Sl1. Pat 7 sts. yf. Sl1. yb. **Turn.**
Next row: Sl1. K5. yf. Sl1. yb. **Turn.**
Next row: Sl1. Pat 3 sts. Break yarn. Slip all sts on left hand needle.

Note: To avoid a hole when knitting a slipped st, pick up the st below the slipped st and slip it onto left-hand needle. Knit this st tog with slipped st above.

With right side of work facing, larger needles and Yellow, pick up and knit 12 sts down Left side of Flap. K41 {**41**-51-**51**} from spare needle. Pick up and knit 12 sts up Right side of Flap. 65 {**65**-75-**75**} sts.
Next row: (Wrong Side). K11. (K1. yo. K1) all in next st. K20 {**20**-25-**25**}. (K1. yo. K1) all in next st. K20 {**20**-25-**25**}. (K1. yo. K1) all in next st. K11.
Next row: P12. (P1. yo. P1) all in next st. P22 {**22**-27-**27**}. (P1. yo. P1) all in next st. P22 {**22**-27-**27**}. (P1. yo. P1) all in next st. P12. Bind off knitwise (**wrong side**).

FINISHING

Pin garment pieces to measurements. Cover with a damp cloth leaving to dry.

Sew shoulder seams.

Collar: With right side of work facing, Bright Blue (for Her) or Green (for Him) and smaller needles, K7 from Right st holder. Pick up and knit 19 {**19**-23-**23**} sts up from Right neck edge. K25 from Back st holder. Pick up and knit 19 {**19**-23-**23**} sts down Left neck edge. K7 from Left st holder. 77 {**77**-85-**85**} sts.
Next row: Knit.
Work 14 {**14**-16-**16**} rows in pat as given for Back, thus ending with right side facing for next row. Place first set of markers at each end of last row.

Cord Casing: Next row: With Yellow, knit.
Work 9 rows in reverse stocking st, thus ending with right side facing for next row. Place second set of markers at each end of last row.
Work 14 {**14**-16-**16**} rows in stocking st. Fasten off loosely.
Sew marked rows tog on **wrong side** to form casing.

Zipper Edging: With right side of work facing, smaller needles and Red (for Her) or Bright Blue (for Him), pick up and knit 11 {**11**-13-**13**} sts down Left Collar edge, below Cord Casing. Pick up and knit 27 {**30**-33-**37**} sts down Left zipper opening. K1 from safety pin. Pick up and knit 27 {**30**-33-**37**} sts up Right zipper opening. Pick up and knit 11 {**11**-13-**13**} sts up Right Collar edge to Cord Casing. 77 {**83**-93-**101**} sts. Bind off.

Sew zipper in position under edging. Fold collar along sewn row and sew in position to **wrong side**. Sew Flap as shown in picture.

Thread elastic through bottom cord casing and adjust to fit. Sew ends of elastic tog.

Twisted Cord (short): (make 2). Cut 4 strands of Red (for Her) or Bright Blue (for Him) 12" long. With all strands tog hold one end and with someone holding other end, twist strands to the right until they begin to curl. Fold the 2 ends tog and tie in a knot so they will not unravel. The strands will now twist themselves tog. Adjust length if desired. Knot into a loop. Sew to bottom sides as shown in picture.

Twisted Cord (long): (make 1). Cut 4 strands of Red (for Her) or Bright Blue (for Him) 38" long. Work as given for Short Twisted Cord. Thread through Collar Cord Casing.

Sew in Sleeves placing rows above markers along bound off sts at armholes of Front and Back to form square armholes. Sew side and sleeve seams.

Twisted Cord

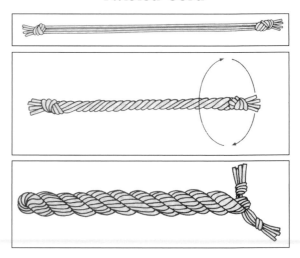

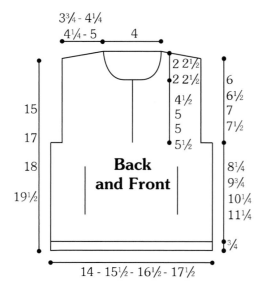

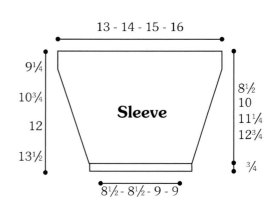

26. Skater Yoke Sweater

Intermediate

SIZES

Bust measurement
Petite	26-28"
Small	30-32"
Medium	34-36"
Large	38-40"

Finished bust
Petite	36"
Small	38½"
Medium	43"
Large	45½"

Size Note: The instructions are written for Petite, with sizes Small, Medium and Large in braces { }. Instructions will be easier to read if you circle all the numbers pertaining to your size. If only one number is given, it applies to all sizes.

MATERIALS

Worsted Weight Yarn:
3½ oz (223 yds/100g)

Sizes	P	S	M	L	
Soft Blue	3	3	3	4	balls
Pink	3	3	3	3	balls
Soft Green	1	1	1	1	ball
White	1	1	1	1	ball
Medium Blue	1	1	1	1	ball

Sample made with **Patons Classic Merino Wool.**

Sizes 6 (3.75 mm) and 7 (4.5 mm) circular knitting needle 24" long. Sets of four size 6 (3.75 mm) and 7 (4.5 mm) double-pointed needles **or size needed for gauge.** 4 st holders.

GAUGE SWATCH

20 sts and 26 rows = 4" with larger needles in stocking st.

Note: Body is worked in one piece to armholes. When working from charts, carry yarn not in use loosely across **wrong side** of work but never over more than 5 sts. When it must pass over more than 5 sts, weave it over and under color in use on next st or at center point of sts it passes over. The colors are never twisted around one another.

BODY

With smaller circular needle and Pink, cast on 180 {**192**-208-**220**} sts. Join in round and placing a marker on first st, proceed as follows:

1st rnd: *K2. P2. Rep from * to end of rnd.
Rep last rnd for (K2. P2) ribbing for 2", inc 0 {**0**-8-**8**} sts evenly across last rnd. 180 {**192**-216-**228**} sts.

Change to larger needle and knit 2 rnds.

Work Chart XIX to end of chart reading rnds from **right** to left, noting the 12 st rep will be worked 15 {**16**-18-**19**} times. *Chart XIX is shown on page 130.*

With Soft Blue, cont even until work from beg measures 15 {**16½**-16½-**17**}".

Next rnd: K6. Slip these 6 sts and last 6 sts of previous rnd onto a st holder (12 sts on holder). K90 {**96**-108-**114**}. Slip last 12 sts just worked onto second st holder. Knit to end of rnd.

SLEEVES

With Pink and set of four smaller needles, cast on 40 {**44**-48-**52**} sts. Divide these sts onto 3 needles: 13 {**15**-16-**17**} sts on 1st and 2nd needles and 14 {**14**-16-**18**} sts on 3rd needle. Join in rnd and placing a marker on first st, work 2" in (K2. P2) ribbing as given for body and inc 8 {**4**-0-**8**} sts evenly on last rnd. 48 {**48**-48-**60**} sts.

Change to set of four larger needles and knit 2 rnds.

Work Chart XIX to end of chart reading rnds from **right** to left, noting the 12 st rep will be worked 4 {**4**-4-**5**} times.

With Soft Blue, cont knitting in rnds inc 1 st beg and end of next and every following 4th rnd until there are 76 {**82**-88-**92**} sts.

Cont even until work from beg measures 16½ {**17½**-18½-**18½**}".

Next rnd: K6. Slip these 6 sts and last 6 sts of previous rnd onto a st holder (12 sts on holder). Break yarn leaving a 12" end for grafting.

YOKE

With Soft Blue and larger circular needle, *knit across 64 {**70**-76-**80**} sts of sleeve. Knit across 78 {**84**-96-**102**} sts of Body. Rep from * once more. Mark last st as end of rnd. 284 {**308**-344-**364**} sts.
Next rnd: *K140 {**152**-170-**89**}. K2tog. Rep from * around. 282 {**306**-342-**360**} sts.

Work Chart XX to end of chart reading rnds from **right** to left, noting the 6 st rep will be worked 47 {**51**-57-**60**} times. *Chart XX is shown on page 30.*

Sizes P, S and M only: Next rnd: With Pink, *K139 {**49**-169}. K2tog. Rep from * around. 280 {**300**-340} sts.

All Sizes: With Pink, work 1 {**5**-5-**6**} rnds even.

Work Chart XXI to end of chart reading rnds from **right** to left, noting the 20 st rep will be worked 14 {**15**-17-**18**} times. 112 {**120**-136-**144**} sts. *Chart XXI is shown on page 118.*

Next 2 rnds: With Pink, knit.

Next rnd: *With Soft Green, K12 {**13**-15-**16**}. K2tog. Rep from * around. 104 {**112**-128-**136**} sts. Work 1 {**1**-1-**2**} rnd(s) even.

With Pink, work 1 {**2**-4-**5**} rnd(s) even.
Next rnd: *With A, K11 {**12**-14-**15**}. K2tog. Rep from * around. 96 {**104**-120-**128**} sts.

Neckband: Change to set of four smaller needles and work 3" in (K2. P2) ribbing. Bind off in ribbing.

Graft Sleeves at underarms (see Diagram).
Pin to measurements and cover with a damp cloth leaving to dry on garment.

Grafting

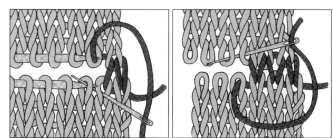